Will the *Death of Us* be the Death *of Me?*

By

Michelle Lorraine

Edited by Lil Barcaski

Published by: GWN Publishing
www.GWNPublishing.com

Cover Design: Kristina Conatser

ISBN: 978-1-959608-99-8

DEDICATION

For those in the throes of a painful divorce, this book is dedicated to you. May you find comfort, resilience, and the courage to heal.

If I Can Stop One Heart From Breaking
Emily Dickinson

If I can stop one heart from breaking,
I shall not live in vain;

If I can ease one life the aching,
Or cool one pain,

Or help one fainting robin
Unto his nest again,
I shall not live in vain.

TABLE OF CONTENTS

ENDORSEMENTS

"Michelle's book really impacted me. It came to me in divine time as I was navigating my own separation. Michelle was a client. I was contracted to help her use her book as an evergreen sales asset for her powerful programmes that help people navigate covert narcissism in gray divorce. To be honest, I'd never really believed in this psychology before Michelle's book. I mean, for there to be a perpetrator of narcissism, there has to be a victim, and I don't buy into victim consciousness. However, Michelle's book helped me see and understand the very intentional and malicious chipping away of a spouse's confidence, self-esteem and even, responsibilities, so that their ownership of everything within the marriage is taken away. The manipulation that goes alongside that is not seen until you are out of the marriage because of the aforementioned lack of confidence and self-esteem, etc.! Reading Michelle's story and insight helped me see and understand my own situation a lot better and I resonated deeply with the feeling that Michelle described... "Feeling like you are going to die." While my situation was certainly very different to Michelle's in that I was ready and an equal part in my marriage dissolving, Michelle helped me see and understand how we had got to that place. She empowered me in the legalities of my separation process and was a key reason I asked for and received what I had contributed to our marriage. The movement that Michelle is leading is POWERFUL. Her tools, resources and

connections are priceless. I am extremely blessed to be helping her to bring all this to more people!"

Clare Williamson

What a remarkable book this is! Life changer for anyone going through the terrifying challenges of divorce, after decades of marriage. Michelle is the voice of experience, wisdom and empathy. A must read for anyone contemplating on getting a divorce or is in the middle of a stressful and confusing situation. This book will help divorcees face this life transition with confidence and optimism.

Ferlie Almonte, Resilience & Confidence Authority

I wish I had read this book and had met Michelle before I had to deal with my very contentious divorce. Working with someone like Michelle would have saved me a world of heartache and financial loss. You don't have to go it alone.

Gina M.

Being a child that her parents divorced later on in life, I found Will the Death of Us Be the Death of Me *very informative and therapeutic to my own personal healing. The author writes about her own struggles with what she terms as "Grey Divorce" and I found myself relating to what she went through because I began to understand what my own parents went through themselves. The sense of commonality that the book evokes gives the reader the sense that they are not alone.*

Divorce is and can be a very difficult time to those who are in the just of this life altering event so having someone guide you by talking about their own experience is a life line because it shows that we can find comfort in another's struggles.

Tina Laurelli

Michelle Lorraine has written a masterful book to help guide any woman going through Wife Abandonment Syndrome. Will the Death of Us be the Death of Me *is chock full of not only her personal story and journal entries but also dozens of resources (including financial), vocabulary definitions, theory explanations and even action items that will get you moving towards recovery. Extensively researched, the author takes you by the hand and walks you through everything you need to know to get up on top of the confusion and heartbreak of an unexpected divorce. It's like a fascinating university course on divorce recovery given by a very heartfelt caring professor!*

Vikki Stark, MSW, Psychotherapist | Author, *Runaway Husbands: The Abandoned Wife's Guide to Recovery and Renewal*, www.runawayhusbands.com

WILL THE DEATH OF US BE THE DEATH OF ME?

INTRODUCTION

> GRAY DIVORCE DEFINITION: *Gray divorce is a term usually referencing divorces in couples who are 50 years old and older and have been in long-term marriages.*

Journal Entry
September 20, 2022

*I am grateful my husband loves me no matter what and for our wonderful trip together to Washington.

*Happy to be rebuilding our relationship with our kids.

*Excited for this promotion for Matthew and so glad to go home to New Jersey to see all our family and friends and rebuild those relationships.

On this very day, he communicated for the first time in 30 years to the girl he had a crush on since high school on his promotion announcement on LinkedIn.

One month later, I got the call.

"I love you, but I'm not in love with you anymore."

In the busy hum of everyday life, a single phone call shattered my world. In the blink of an eye, the life I knew or thought I knew crumbled, leaving me at the crossroads of heartbreak and resilience.

Since the day I got that phone call from my husband of more than 30 years, letting me know my marriage and life as I understood it was over, I have learned a lot. Particularly about the secretive and intricate relationship between the covert narcissist and empaths (codependents).

If you are not familiar with the term "covert narcissist," they are people who crave admiration and importance. They lack empathy and often act in a different way than the overt narcissist we think of when we think of narcissism such as having fantasies about fame or glory and exaggerating -abilities. Not having these more common issues can make it hard to realize what you are dealing with because they can hide the more obvious signs. But they can be just as destructive.

The empath has a tendency to be the target for these people. Empaths have the unique ability to take on another's perspective. They understand and feel the other person's experience at a deep level. This can lead them to becoming codependent on someone who craves attention and seems to need them on all levels.

I have met many other women who experienced the exact discard, and unexpected to me, men who also are in the throes of painful divorces and coming to terms with being in a relationship for years with a covert narcissist and never realized it.

Most of us would admit we didn't see it coming. I certainly didn't! Everybody wanted to be us. We were the love story everybody looked to. Most people liked my husband, and as a young man, he was a good student, good-looking, tall, and athletic. I believe he aged semi-gracefully, and so did I. We owned beautiful homes and expensive cars, went on lavish vacations, and seemed truly happy.

Every discarded woman (and man) I've talked to has the same story. None expected anything other than to grow old with the partner they slept next to, lived with, and loved for more than half their lives. Until that phone call, or in some cases, texts, and even a few cases I have heard of, a letter left on the dresser or kitchen table saying, "It's over." *Discarded.* That's the word you will come to understand and that it happened to you. It's shocking, traumatizing, embarrassing, callous and unexpected.

If this resonates with you, has happened to you, or describes someone you know and care about, this book is for you or them. Is someone you know going through this? A sister, dear friend, aunt, mother, or even one of the men in your life might be dealing with a covert narcissist. I know there were warning signs I either didn't see or didn't want to see. My name was not on any of our finances. He was in a bad mood whenever I was in a good mood and vice versa. He found subtle ways to control every aspect of my life. He made himself the good guy with our daughter, and that made me the bad one. One day, I was dancing around the kitchen, making dinner. I was happily cooking while he sat across from me at the counter. I looked up suddenly, realizing that he was staring at me. "What is it?" I asked, smiling still. "Do I have something on my face?"

"It's too bad your daughter hates you," he replied. "You were such a good mom."

Deflated. That was all it took to destroy my good mood.

Gaslighting was the kind of thing he would do so that he could control the situation. He would get me upset, console me, and tell me to lie down and rest. "I'm just going to go play a little golf. I'll be back later with a nice dinner for us." Then he would escape, and I would retreat to our bedroom with a pounding headache and a broken spirit. This way, he could exit to go where he wanted, do what he wanted, and not have to explain where he was going. Later, he would return like the hero, and I would fall into his "loving" arms for consolation.

I had no authority as a parent with my child. She would turn to him for everything. He set things up so that I was always the bad guy. He had control of the money. All good things come from Dad, right? He was the provider, the giver of everything, not me. I could not discipline her or even win an argument. She would call Daddy any time she was upset with me, who would tell her to wait for him to come home. Then, he would sit us down and decide how to deal with the situation as if I were just another child.

Often, the man is in control of the money, as it was in my marriage. Women trust them and they don't realize how much he is hiding from them, or they can become the target for scams. I have met women who even had their businesses stolen at the end by their spouse, who wound up selling the business they built to some friend or cousin. They trusted their husbands and let them have control of all the finances. This leads to disaster.

Most of the women I have met who have been discarded were living big lifestyles just like we were. All of a sudden, they were broke. The husband was done with them and the money was no longer accessible to them. This abrupt change of lifestyle is jarring and takes a whole lot of adjustment. My husband told me to go get a job after 31 years of marriage and finally earn a living. The courts make women sound like they are lazy because they didn't work when in reality they've been running the household, caring for children, and taking care of all the details of life.

I felt like I was on trial for murder at our divorce hearing. My lawyer explained that we had moved about every three years for his business. I ran our households, took care of everything in our homes and for our family, and relocated nationally five times faithfully. When was I supposed to get a career? I had many jobs but no time for a career. What kind of job could I do now after being out of the workforce for more than 30 years and in my 50s?

The beginning of the end for us started when our daughter was going through some serious trauma in 2009 and needed therapy. His answer to how we would deal with this was to drink more. We were always social drinkers but not to excess. Suddenly, we were drinking wine every night, often polishing off an entire bottle or more. I started to realize I was numbing myself. Things were starting to unravel, and I think I may have seen the hand-writing on the wall.

So, I did something unusual in 2021. I went to AA. Mind you, I was not what you think of when you think of an alcoholic. I was not a day drinker, nor did I drink alone. In fact, overall I was not someone who drank too much. There was some history of alco-holism in my family, and I saw myself slipping. My husband, and many of our friends, were surprised. But I saw it as a crutch, and I would keep that crutch if I kept on drinking. So, I stopped, and when my head cleared, I started to see things as they really were.

As I got healthier, the game got too hard for him. He needed someone with attachment issues and a deep need for codependency. The covert narcissist is passive-aggressive. They need someone to control and that person has to need them too to be controlled. Something in them from childhood needs this kind of relationship. But still, I didn't see this coming. I didn't think my getting stronger would create the outcome that we came to. It came out of the blue for me, and it took a lot of healing, and still does, to be able to look back and see the path we were on that would lead to the end of us.

I was slowly waking up to the reality that I was in a co-abusive relationship with a covert narcissist, and I had no idea how to get out of it, protect myself, and begin to recover... YES, how to recover from my 32-year marriage.

I HAD NO IDEA WHAT HAPPENED TO ME.

How did I not see it and my part in it?

What to do next!

Being discarded is traumatizing. There are so many women in my situation, and not enough people are talking about it because it is embarrassing. This is not just a story of abandonment and discard; it's a journey through the wreckage, a search for strength in the unexpected, and a testament to the power of rebuilding when the ground beneath you gives way. As I navigated the challenging journey of unexpected discard, I found myself in search of answers and guidance that seemed elusive. The information I sought to understand what happened to me and the new arena I was in was very hard to come by. I found as many books as I could on all the topics and read and listened to them all. I worked with a therapist weekly for a year. He was the first person to explain that I was experiencing financial abuse as well as emotional. Just because there was no physical abuse didn't mean abuse wasn't happening.

I joined 12-step programs and recovery classes.

I found people on TikTok who specialized in the nooks and crannies of some of my needs and took classes and seminars.

I watched all the YouTube videos.

Joined all the support groups on Facebook. (Every day, these groups get 50 new women members.)

There are some important lessons I want to share with people going through this kind of gray divorce that are important to learn. If you don't learn this stuff, you will be kept as SUPPLY to be pulled back in and released again for constant abuse. For starters, if you are numbing yourself with alcohol, pot, or any drug for that matter, stop drinking and getting high. Get your mind clear, or you will never get to the other side of it. You have to deal with the discard head on. Mind you, I am not saying that if your doctor puts you on depression or anxiety meds, that you should ignore that. Ask if you need it!!! Do what your doctor recommends. But as your mind clears, you can start to see what you have to do. Too many women I know are drinking to excess to not feel the pain of all of this. Don't fall into the same trap with the next person. You will be worse off than you were before. You will likely meet other men or women just like the one you left. Many men are looking for a purse or a nurse. There are predatory men (and I'm sure some women too) who are looking for someone with money or who are healthy and can take care of them when they are sick and old.

A friend of mine is going through a divorce similar to mine from a man much like my ex. She called me and said, "I met a terrific guy online. I'm going to drive upstate to meet with him. He makes me feel safe and like I'm home."

My answer to her and any of you saying that. "Run!" You will learn that this is a red flag.

She was being sucked in by someone who knew what she wanted to hear, so he told her all the things that would get her to trust him. This kind of behavior is learned when young. The covert narcissist discovers the way to manipulate people to make them believe that they are the answer to all their problems, and that they will keep them safe if they just do what they ask or give them what they need. Gaslighting is a big thing with the covert narcissist. Overtly narcissistic people are easily spotted, and you stay away from them. I think coverts are formed at an early age due to unmet needs. They learn to be passive-aggressive to get what they want. With a lot of self-discovery and learning to love and care for yourself, you eventually begin to have the confidence to see when you are being snowed.

WHY I AM WRITING THIS BOOK

You might wonder why I would open up and share what I've gone through. In truth, I feel that it's part of my recovery to document this and build something that will allow me to help other people going through something similar. I am creating Gray Divorce Support Group, and I will be speaking to women's recovery groups. I have lost a lot of friends and family through this. All the LOSS! Our old couple friends are shocked and repeat, "He will be back when he realizes the grass is not greener" or "He has to have had a brain aneurysm!"

I know what kind of pain this brings. I want to be a resource for other people, especially women like me who have been tossed aside after decades of marriage. I want to help women like me get to the other side of this insanely difficult time in their lives. I am working on other books and guides to help women navigate some of the things that happen in court, how to deal with the loss of those friends that saw you as the power couple and now treat you like you are a leper, how to deal with your children and their issues, the financial issues, or even on how to work on starting your own business.

Learn who you are.

Create your own space, make new friends, and take your time with relationships and dating. Please don't rush into the same issues. I want you to know you are going to be okay. Take the time to heal and learn to love yourself. You are not domestic labor or a paycheck. You are a vital, wonderful, vibrant person. You deserve to be happy. I am finally rebuilding... ME! I am finding my own real life purpose. I cannot be going through all of this for nothing. I am going through it to help other people in the same boat. I hope that part of why I had to go through all of this was for you!

You are not alone!

WILL THE DEATH OF US BE THE DEATH OF ME?

CHAPTER 1
THE END CAN BE THE BEGINNING

"Hey! I was just thinking about you. I'm kind of sad about the real estate here in Jersey," I said as I answered. Then, I heard my husband hysterically crying on the line and immediately my heart sank. "What's wrong? What Happened?"

I literally just had the best week in my life being back home in New Jersey eating great food, visiting favorite places, and walking the beaches with our dog.

I was under the stress of preparing my home in Montana for sale, driving to Florida from Montana, relocating my mom from Florida to Pennsylvania after losing her trailer in Hurricane Ian, then driving to New Jersey and settling into our home rental. I had been driving for another week scouting home purchasing locations in New Jersey.

Thirty-one years of marriage, and it ended with a phone call.

"I don't want to be married anymore. It's not you. It's me... I just lost the spark."

"I love you, and we are best friends," I answered.

"You don't marry your best friend," he said.

"YES, YOU DO... it's all everyone is looking for; everyone is looking for what we have... our love and commitment to each other."

"No, Michelle. I made up my mind. We will be separated for two years and then get divorced."

"Do I get a lawyer?" I asked.

"NO! You do not need a lawyer."

"Is there someone else?"

"NO!" he said. "But I will probably date."

"What about Carly (his dog)?"

"You keep her."

"Are you okay? Are you dying and don't want me to care for you?" At this point, I was frantic and grabbing at straws.

"No, I have been feeling this for as long as I can remember."

"Does it have anything to do with our daughter?"

"No! Nothing to do with her... It's me. It's not you!!" he repeated.

THAT WAS ALL A LIE. But I would not find out how much of a lie—just how bad things were—for a full year later. I had no idea who I was married to for 31 years, and the vengeful delight he would get from hurting me more than I had ever been hurt in my life. The very person that I loved and adored set out to destroy me.

Looking back, I should have considered how much Matthew's childhood was marked by turmoil and hardship. When he was just two years-old, his father, who had been unfaithful to his mother and living with another women, died in a car accident, leaving his mother to raise two boys on her own.

Matthew and his older brother, born 18 months apart, faced a difficult upbringing. His brother was often violent and abusive towards both their mother and Matthew, creating a tense and hostile home environment. In response to the chaos around him, Matthew learned to manipulate his mother as a means of navigating the emotional challenges he faced and to gain a semblance of control over his unpredictable world.

I am not a physiologist but I believe this tumultuous start to his early life set up his future behavior. Our childhoods often reflect who we become as adults and affect how we handle life situations. In my opinion, this is not an excuse for Matthew's behavior or for how he treated me but it sheds some light on how he became the man he became and how he handles stressful situations.

We met in a restaurant where I worked, and it was a fast and furious love affair in the summer of 1990. He was tall and cute. He was having dinner with my manager after they played basketball earlier that day, and I was ending my shift when my manager called me over to introduce me to the table of guys. Our eyes locked and fireworks exploded. We were together since that moment, immediately addicted to each other. I was under the impression that we were both 23 years old. I later found out his real age was 20.

That summer we spent every night together, usually out partying at a bar or friend's house parties. He was working all over Pennsylvania but did whatever he could to be home and pick me up every night. He had ended a high school long-term relationship, and I was fresh out of an engagement and looking to find myself.

As summer was winding down and everyone was preparing to return to college, I had no plans but to continue to waitress. A recruiter from the Air Force was working on me to enlist and I tested in as a mechanic, but a friend who contracted with the Army stressed that they promise you everything and give you nothing. He invited me to go to Hawaii with him where he and some friends had started a business. He suggested I come along and see if I like it. He was a much older man but we had friends in common who went out with us a few times.

I talked with my family, and he talked to my family, and I discussed it with my boyfriend. It all seemed to be a plan for the time being, the stipulation by my grandmother being that I purchase an open-ended return ticket and my boyfriend would come the following summer. So, off to Oahu and goodbye to Pennsylvania. Little did I know that this was the worst plan I could ever have made and that the repercussions will haunt me until the day I die.

Once in Hawaii, I realized very quickly that I was, in a way, kidnapped with my family's and my permission. We ended up in a remote part of Oahu in Waihee in an apartment in the offseason with no phone, car, or friends. This older man, let's call him Brad, worked as a roofer, not the owner of a roofing company as he had told my family. I was isolated. I had been sick since I arrived and assumed that it was a travel sickness. When I went to the doctor, I found out I was pregnant. I reached my grandmother by borrowing a neighbor's phone, (there were no cell phones in 1990) and told her I was pregnant.

"Honey, thank God! I found out that Brad is married and he abandoned his wife and four children," she told me. "He sold their car and took all their money." I froze. The neighbors asked what was happening. I told them what my grandmother had said, and we called to schedule a flight home to get me out of there as fast as possible.

When I confronted Brad, he said that he was separated and she was crazy. I knew he was lying and trying to manipulate me into staying. I left Oahu to return home never to see or hear from Brad again.

Returning from Hawaii now pregnant, my life and the world were heading in a different direction. The Gulf War was just beginning, and I was going to keep and have my baby as a single unmarried mother with no job and no insurance. I did not know how but my grandmother said she would help, and I went into a pregnancy center which helped me sort out my feelings and mind and referred me to support. I applied for public assistance. Alone and scared, I joined a Bible study group, became a Christian, and started to build my life. Before my boyfriend returned to college, we met and I told him I was pregnant, carrying his child. He lifted me, spun me around, and said, "Now I have you!" At the time I thought this was such a loving statement but after learning about covert narcissism I now know I was in his lair.

He had continued to party all along, wrecking a friend's car, and his court troubles emptied his parent's 401k. He headed back to college to continue the same bad behavior. I did not want him to have the pressure of needing to be a part of this life, so I freed him to do as he wanted and he did. When home on break, he was partying heavily. I wrote to him and told him this was not the life I wanted for myself and my baby as it was my life growing up and I wanted to do better. He chose to complete the last semester of college and then decided to come home and get a job stating that he wanted to prove he could be a good boyfriend.

> ### Journal Entry
> *February 6, 1991*
>
> Becoming a Christian, my life has changed and I don't want to live the life I had as a child. I want our child to have better. I will never stop you from being a part of your child's life, but I want more than drugs and instability.

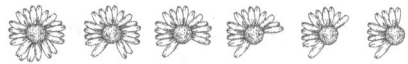

We worked hard. He was working full time and I went to college while living with family, and then we eventually found our own apartment. Being a Christian, I suggested we marry, and he agreed. We married when our daughter was three-months-old.

She had complications at birth and later developed a cataract in her left eye. He abandoned me for every doctor appointment, every surgery (except the last one), but most importantly the days and nights of having to patch her eye and work with her being scared and uncomfortable. He was gone... working overtime.

Once I asked him to come home during the first patching and painful drops for our daughter because it was so hard on me. He came home and said he could not stay. He cried and left to go party with a friend and his girlfriend from fire school. My daughter cried because daddy cried and she thought that I made him cry.

This is where the division between her and I began. If she was upset, he would tell her to wait until he came home and he would manage it. He would sit us at the table and ask, "Okay, what happened?" like we were both children, completely undermining my authority with our daughter.

We have friends who worked in a new industry that were trying to get him a position, and he got that position after two years of waiting. During that time, there were many red flags I overlooked because of church suggestions and trying to be a good wife and mother. He would disappear with friends after work. When he went to Texas for training, I was worried because of how secretive he always was, but he always just said I was insecure and did not need to worry about strip clubs and other women. He got to Texas and disappeared for four days. He had stolen hundreds of dollars and hid it in his locker at work (I had a grocery envelope of money that needed to last all month to the penny and it was mostly gone). He went to a strip club and apparently went farther than the rest of the group. His boss said, "your wife is going to kill you." I later found out what had happened on the trip.

He got a tattoo that covered half of his back and went to spring break parties. He never called and missed his daughter's fifth birthday. I felt so bad that I wrapped a book, put it in a box, and pretended it was shipped from him in Texas. To this day, she does not know it was me that sent that prized possession.

I picked him up at the airport and was humiliated that I was lied to, and also because of what he did. The other wives knew what happened and said, "I could not tell you because you are so jealous." That made me so insecure in myself and convinced me that I needed to work on myself.

It took a long time to forgive him for this, and my father told me I couldn't because it was not about me. I am confused because my husband was a liar. (He should know. He was a liar too.)

The new job changed our lives forever due to pay increases and benefits and eventually promotions that would take us to Louisiana. Our daughter was in 2nd grade and we missed our family so much, but we did it for the betterment of our family's future. This also was a choice that would hurt me in the future as I trusted my husband and his whole plan was to use us to get to an end and leave me. I was very close with my mom and Grandmother and found an entry in my journal where I said that he came home from work and told me I could not call home anymore. He said that the phone bill was up 50 dollars because of my calls home. As the good wife, I agreed but I missed my family so much and became more isolated. My daughter and my relationship was very strained at this time as we spent all our time together. She had a hard time making friends, and we were stressed. She hated me at this point.

I never really knew why but I have learned that living with a covert narcissist and empath is horrible for a child. I was told by her for years I was a narcissist and an abuser, and I ruined her father's life. In this situation, the child needs to attack the other parent to gain the attention of the covert narcissist.... and many years later the two would join forces to try to destroy me.

My father died. I went home for the funeral, and I never returned to Louisiana because my husband interviewed during the trip home for the funeral and accepted a job in New Jersey.

For years, my therapist would tell me to, "retreat and protect myself." A fight would start over something and my daughter would scream at me to try to get me to engage and scream back. I would leave the house and go sit in my car crying until my husband came home and magically all was okay.

A few years later, on a shopping trip for my now teenaged daughter before her cruise with friends, she was angry that I only bought her two bathing suits and not the three she wanted. While she yelled all the way to the car about her allowance, I explained why we were only giving her money weekly (she was caught with pot). In the car, the fight continued and she tried to jump out of the moving car. I grabbed her shirt and held her until I pulled over. We got home and she ran to her friend's home, saying that I tried to throw her out of the car. She even went to the police station to report me. The marks on her neck were her fingernail marks that went straight down and were clearly not made by me. She refused to come home and the accusations began. At school, she told every teacher we abused her and her friends told her that if she could prove it, she could live in juvenile hall and we would have to pay for her expenses until she was 24-years-old. Later, a judge told her that was a terrible plan and not what she thought to be true. Her friends had misled her on all of that.

She punched out the windows in my garage, wiped blood on her face, and called the police. By the time my husband got home from work, the police had me in my kitchen asking me if I like to hit children. The paramedic came in and said the wounds were self-inflicted and that she had wiped her own blood on her face and had a boxer break from punching something. At that point, our daughter needed intense in-patient therapy, and she was checked in away from us to get help. My husband got to be the hero in all of this and I became the bad guy. He brought home wine and said we would drink every night and that's how we handled her being away.

Never once did it ever come up in therapy that I was with a covert narcissist because I spoke of him on the sidelines and all the focus was on me being a horrible mom who just wanted to be better.

RESOURCES

- BOOK: *It's Not You,* by Dr Ramani Duriasola

VOCABULARY:

DISCARD: Narcissistic discard refers to a pattern of behavior exhibited by individuals with narcissistic personality disorder (NPD) when they abruptly end a relationship or discard someone who was once a source of narcissistic supply. This is the last phase of the narcissistic love pattern. Narcissistic discard is usually not a peaceful or gentle process. It can be sudden and unexpected, leaving the partner devastated and abandoned.

CONTENTIOUS DIVORCE: refers to a divorce process characterized by significant conflict and disagreement between the spouses. In a contentious divorce, the parties may struggle to agree on various important issues such as:

DIVISION OF ASSETS AND PROPERTY: Disputes over how to fairly divide marital property, assets, and debts.

CHILD CUSTODY AND SUPPORT: Conflicts regarding the custody and visitation rights of children, as well as the amount and terms of child support.

ALIMONY OR SPOUSAL SUPPORT: Disagreements over whether one spouse should provide financial support to the other and the amount and duration of such support.

OTHER FINANCIAL MATTERS: Disputes related to pensions, retirement accounts, and other financial matters.

A contentious divorce often involves more legal proceedings, such as court hearings and trials, compared to an uncontested or amicable divorce where both parties can reach an agreement with minimal conflict. This type of divorce can be emotionally draining, time-consuming, and expensive due to the legal fees and extended duration of the process.

ACTION ITEM:

☐ Visit this website: https://rebootrecovery.com/

☐ Consider this program: *Trauma Reboot: Trauma healing for Everyone,* by Evan and Jenny Owens

Narcissist Discard

Narcissist discard is a phase in the narcissistic abuse cycle where the narcissist distances themselves from or ends a relationship once they no longer perceive the other person as useful or fulfilling their needs.

Examples	Coping
Emotional withdrawal: become distant, cold, or unresponsive.	**Acceptance:** Acknowledge the reality of the situation & accept that discard has occurred.
Devaluation: criticize, belittle, or demean the other person.	**Avoid falling into a "rescue" mindset:** Resist the urge to fix the relationship or save the narcissist.
Silent treatment: ignoring or refusing to engage with the other person	**Set boundaries:** limiting or cutting off contact

simplypsychology.org

WILL THE DEATH OF US BE THE DEATH OF ME?

CHAPTER 2

WAS IT EVER OK?

Journal Entry

Ramblings on my mind:

I was constantly saying, "I did not say..." "I did not do..." and asking him "why are you angry all the time?" and, "Why do you give me the middle finger constantly rubbing your eye, nose, and face with it?"

You said that you were happy with me in my counseling and therapy, but I could tell that you were so angry at me because I was developing boundaries and you were losing control over me and it was wearing you down.

We had no one else because you did not want friends, just us, but I fought to bring my mom with us. You're jealous of my friends Nicole, Ellen, and Angel... you lied to me constantly and I did not know you know because I had to ask 500 questions to get to the real answer. The same question from a different angle would finally get me the right answer. You willingly withheld information from me.

You always thought that I was too nice and hated my free will and would put me down for the very things you said you loved about me.

You had no boundaries with other women and had different personas with different groups of people. To make fun of my spirituality, you became "Father Matt" on Sundays at golf and would hold church on each hole, "drinking the blood and eating the body."

You withheld intimacy from me for years under the guise that it was your health, and I have found your paperwork and there is no reason given for you to do that to me.

Buying cars without telling me but not allowing me access to funds over monthly bills.

I don't know how I did not see, but I am glad I am out and can now see.

Despite four relocations later to New Jersey, California, New Orleans, and Montana, we experienced life like everyone else. Life was full of family sicknesses, problems with our child, family deaths, and growing pains in our relationship. During the most recent relocation, while I was waiting in New Jersey for our sixth relocation, I received the call. It was a Saturday morning in October of 2022 stating, "I love you, but I'm not in love with you!" And that was it.

My father-in-law stated that my husband had mental issues in his family medical history and hoped he would come to his senses. Matthew would never admit this nor would he hear of engaging in any kind of therapy for himself. That might imply weakness or imperfection, something a narcissist would never allow for.

At that point, I was done, because he had abandoned me years earlier in 2012 when he "did not know if he wanted to be married anymore." My in-laws took care of me for a month back then while I recovered from that news. I vowed that rebuilding after that was the one and only time I would ever do that, and now I wish I never had.

He always had other women. I don't know if he had an actual affair, but there were always other "work wives," and specific waitresses and bartenders he would go and see. Once at a neighborhood party, there was a gentleman there that I did not know and the two of them went off to talk oddly. Later, I asked Matthew what they were talking about and he said, "Oh, he was telling me he spent a lot of time near where my work is and was telling me how to pick-up bartenders, and that they are the easiest to access." I flipped out. His mask slipped that night, but because we were both out of a party and drinking, that's how it got washed away.

He also had a "work wife," Helen, and she was the worst... texting between the both of them was nonstop and he would answer even during sex with me. I can remember once at a Christmas party, she walked up to me and said, "I need him now." They sat down at our table and talked for over an hour. I was so upset I went outside and called a friend. When I came back, I stood there like *are you done with my husband yet* and that became an argument.

Since we met, there was always one girl—Beverly—who he was obsessed with in high school, and even when she had a boyfriend, he would walk to her house from his house just to see her. So, all through our marriage, from the very beginning, she was the girl that he never got to have. And you know what? That's who he left me for. After the phone call where he said he didn't love me anymore, I started searching social media to try to understand what had happened. I found a post on LinkedIn where she congratulated him and underneath it, he replied, "Beverly, how's life? Long time no see."

I knew something about this was suspicious.

I didn't know the truth until eight months later during the depositions. He felt that that was going to be the big bomb to drop to devastate me. He bought a house with her, and he was living with her three months after leaving our 31-year marriage. In court, he accused me of being able to have a career because he didn't want me to have any of the money that we've earned during the marriage. He believed he earned it, not me, and I should not be entitled to any of it. My lawyer asked if the new girlfriend was working and he said, "No, she's not working."

What did she do? She was at home remodeling a house and taking care of sick parents, my exact previous role.

Through all of these instances, I was made to feel like I was insecure and jealous, which made me feel like crap. Being accused of being abusive almost killed me. I always thought that I was a strong, attractive, proud woman, but over time, it just broke me down. My daughter saw this and, of course, she was going to think I am the jealous insecure one in the family.

I have been in therapy for 25 years trying to fix those things. Never once did a therapist pick up on the fact that I may be in some type of an abusive relationship. No one ever hit me. I had a nice house and a decent car. The closest I have ever come to being physically hurt was the very last time before the discard as the mask was slipping. It was during the last six months that we were together. The last time we had sex, he put his hands around my neck and I don't remember him squeezing, but I remember the pressure. I opened my eyes, scared, and looked at him, and his face looked evil. He jumped up out of bed and slammed into the wall. And I was like, "What in the hell is happening? What just happened? What was that?" He never gave an answer, just nonstop avoidance as always.

One of the last days before I had to leave for Florida, after working a month on getting the house ready to pack and ship to New Jersey, I was standing in the kitchen humming a bit as I was cooking. I turned around to see that he was glaring at me. I just shook my head and asked, "What is wrong? You're looking at me like you hate me."

"It's a shame your daughter hates you," he answered. "You were such a great mom."

I couldn't believe that in the middle of my normal day cooking dinner, this was what he decided to drop on me standing in the kitchen, glaring at me like he was going to stab me. I said to him, "It doesn't matter what you think and it doesn't matter what I think. It only matters what she thinks." I turned around and went back to my song and cooking. I think that was the beginning of the end because he had lost control over me at that point. I'm so very thankful for being in a 12-step program because it's the one thing that taught me boundaries and that was how I was able to keep my mind straight in that instance and many other instances to come.

Minimization is a constant and terrible tactic used by covert narcissists. They say something to hurt you under the guise of a joke. My husband was very passive-aggressive, especially with his jokes. He could cut me down in public and most would not notice, but I could feel it. He would always be defensive if confronted. "I was only kidding!" Then my daughter would add, "Gosh, you can't take a joke. He's only joking."

Most of the time we had no meaningful conversations, and no deep connections. Mainly, it seemed like a business arrangement.

I assumed I was married to a workaholic, and I used to joke with him and say, "You're like a serial killer. You don't own anything personal. You don't even have anything on your bedside table." The narcissists really don't have a life. In a way, they are gaining that from you. Meanwhile, you're holding on and trying to make sense of what the heck is going on, always trying to be better, and keeping up with things.

Before the first discard, it was Christmas and he asked me what I wanted and one of the things that I listed was socks. I know it's a horrible choice, but I needed socks. I thought it was a joke. But that year, that's all that he got me... socks, hiking socks, sweat socks. He got my daughter a very beautiful sweater, which was curious because he never purchased Christmas gifts for anyone but me, as I did all the gift shopping.

Our whole family was visiting in the house that I had decorated. I had a block party for Christmas for our neighbors. I had his family over the night before for dinner and I had breakfast made. The socks thing felt underhanded and disrespectful and just upset me terribly. My daughter told me, "You are so spoiled. How selfish are you? You got something for Christmas."

He had no idea why I was so upset. The Christmas before this, I was working as a teacher and had off my two weeks of Christmas vacation. I came home and he had gotten a vasectomy without telling me and had some kind of reaction to it. He laid around with ice on his crotch for a week during my only time off.

When he left me the first time, he woke up one morning and was sad. He had been talking to me way less than normal, and he said, "I don't know if I wanna be married anymore." I felt like I had been punched in the face. "All right," I said. "I guess you better figure that out."

He left and shortly thereafter just as Hurricane Sandy was coming. He simply packed up and moved to the office under the pretense that he needed to stay there during the hurricane, but he did not call me. He did not reach out to me. He came home and wanted to eat in the middle of the night and then went back to work. I'm sure he was with Helen the whole time. I was devastated and went to stay with his mother and father, believing I was getting a divorce. I lay in their house and cried for a week with pneumonia. He never called. My friends and coworkers were trying to tell me that I needed to get an understanding of our financial situation.

I went home to do research and look for paperwork. Our daughter was home from boot camp and realized that we were in the middle of a separation. She began to attack me, telling me again how horrible I was. She chased me out of the house and because of the whole, "retreat and protect yourself," I ended up back at my mother and father-in-law's. At that point, I realized I had to get my shit together and be able to go back to my own home.

This became horrible because the only rule he gave her was, "Just don't say 'fuck you' to your mother anymore." That was all she could *not do*, and she left again. He came home suddenly and wanted to work things out, not because he loved me, not because of a new realization, but because he was offered a promotion. He told me, "We're gonna take a relocation to California because you always wanted to live in California, and we can work on our marriage. Don't tell anyone yet." No one could know until it was the right time. What I didn't know was that this would put me in a situation where I wouldn't be able to discuss this move with people and really consider how I felt about it. In hindsight, I wish we would've gotten divorced at that point and I would've stayed in New Jersey. But I went to California hoping we were working together on a second chance. When he called me to discard me the second time in 2022, I remember one of the things that I said to him was, "I knew you would do this to me again." He answered with, "You know me better than I know myself."

Why would I ever stay with somebody who I knew would do this to me... again! It's my biggest regret and hope that it will serve as a lesson to heed for others.

Journal Entries
October 2022, early Discard

A Letter to myself:

Hi Michelle,

I am so sorry you are having a horrible time right now but please remember this too shall pass.

Matthew knows how hard he hit you and knows your life path and still chose to betray you and abandon you. Remember he is a "sick man" and as you grow and heal, he does not have the same ability to do so.

a. This discard could be the biggest blessing in your life and only time will tell. People are coming into your life because you are worthy to have friends and love. So glad you have your pup Carly Jane and a beautiful home in Florida. God loves you and wants the best for you so, "this too shall pass!" It will pass or you will pass :) You are strong and have loved this man so deeply, but he fell out of love and did not want to be married anymore.

b. Right now, the only way out of this despair of being abandoned by Matthew is to end this as quick as I can and to begin to live my life on my own. The very best outcome is that I am financially stable to live and have a fulfilled life. I want my friendships to grow and I want to explore the world. Be with people that love me and like to be with me and have intimacy in my life again.

c. Right now, I fear two things: one is that I am unlovable... I revealed my whole heart and soul to Matthew and he broke it because he did not like me anymore. Two is being poor and needing to struggle to survive because I have no access to finances. Starting a career and a full-time job after giving up a career to forward his career leaves me unqualified at 57 to start over and earn retirement.

d. The trigger of being accused of something again and to confront the imperfect parts of me have left me feeling scared. I choose people that will attack me to get their way, hurt me without remorse, and just leave me as if I never mattered. I try to do good and have made bad choices in my life. I am not happy how this turned out. I loved and adored my husband and wanted the best for all of us and was a solid wife and mother. I really thought I did that. Josh's abuse allegations against us when she was in 9th grade and now Matthew with fraud allegations. I cannot process that this is how my life turned out. I feel that I have paid for stupidity in big ways and will always carry this.

e. I am having a hard time moving on from my part in this. I don't feel like I have ever dealt with how people have hurt me and only focus on my role in the situation. I know this is being cleared so I can heal and start new without taking my past into the future. I cannot allow what they say about me to control me anymore. "What baggage are my ghosts using to haunt me?" I can overcome this. I am in control now!

f. Slut – I was called this by my husband at Oktoberfest in Germany when a man put his hand down the back of my pants at our table and I stopped him. If I was not so nice and stopped acting like a slut, he would not have done that to me.

g. Cunt – I did not deserve this disrespect during an argument we had about our daughter's engagement and upcoming wedding.

h. Sadness - because I never knew he did not love me and only stayed with me for our child and could never commit to me.

i. Grief – for losing something I worked so hard on for so long

j. Anger – to learn that I am meaningless to Matthew and was only used and manipulated by him. I saw red flags but did not know.

k. Guilt - about being young and making decisions about our lives and not having the facilities to be a better informed decision maker.

l. Resentment - For Matthew tricking me into driving to Montana to confront me in person, saying that I hurt him intentionally and his plans for the discard beginning there.

m. The passage of time - emotional work with Dr. Bernstein. "It's never too late to be what you might have been." "Talk to yourself like someone you love." " No shorts cuts to any place worth going."

n. I am on vacation today and finished the covert narcissist book and cannot believe what I have been through and will go through with Matthew. What really happened? It was not all me!! Other people were there and chose to respond with love or hate.

1. *He would never walk the beach with me because his feet hurt.*

2. *I never received a compliment unless I asked.*

3. *He was always sick and miserable on vacations.*

4. *Never pursued, I needed to pursue.*

5. *I planned all things like vacations, holidays, dinners, Christmas presents.*

6. *He told me, hatefully, that my eyes weren't blue anymore and that was what he loved best about me.*

o. Last day before my 56th birthday and all has come forward and laid bare. I am so sorry for my part in this and for the hurt I have caused.

p. I am trusting this was all for a reason and I played what part I was supposed to play. I repent, apologize, and have made amends to change my ways. I am doing the best I can with what God has given me. I could not control others; they have their own free will. I understand now that I was functioning from a place of unhealed traumas and people in my life used me as they needed to for themselves. I trust my higher power will care for me and I will be provided for. I will eat and have a home and places to travel to and friends, lovers, husbands.

q. So stressed by the ups and downs of this divorce's blessing to the right people. I will heal and help others to heal. I will recover and help others to recover. I will love and help others to love. I will trust and help others to trust.

r. Today, I can breathe. I am perfectly and wonderfully made in the image of my higher power. I am not sick. I am only acting out in pain and hurt. Thankful for healing thoughts and knowledge.

s. I need to get educated in this divorce process. Confused by the lawyer telling me to approve extraordinary spending and when I did, my lawyer changed the amount and Matthew denied it and now, we are filing another motion. So confused.

t. So stressed by the ups and downs of this divorce process, my identity stolen along with 10K from savings, it makes me sick to my stomach. I need to find a coach or advisor to help with this. I need to get ready for mediation.

u. I hate you, Matthew. I cannot believe you of all people chose to hurt me like this. You are mean and insane. Kyle and Brenda both said that you were mean and distant at work and treat people horribly. I had no idea that was who you are. You have been horrible to me and I thought it was because of your health, but it's just that you have been plotting this for years (2012 -2022). Why did you keep me, the "slut/cunt?" You hated me and I was beginning to heal and see it for the first time. "Two years and then I am gone!" Where am I going Matthew? Where are you going? I got a lawyer and I am going to build my life in a way that you will never hurt me again. You are a sick man, Matthew J. (gone no contact).

RESOURCES

BOOKS

- *Runaway Husbands Runaway Husbands: The Abandoned Wife's Guide to Recovery and Renewal,* by Vikki Stark
- *In Sheep's Clothing: Understanding and Dealing with Manipulative People,* by George K. Simon Jr. Ph.D.

VOCABULARY:

Hallmarks of Wife Abandonment Syndrome, By Vikki Stark

Do you suspect that you're a victim of Wife Abandonment Syndrome? Here are the ten defining characteristics that will let you know if you are. You don't need to check off all ten to fit the definition.

- Prior to the separation, the husband had seemed to be an attentive, emotionally engaged spouse, looked upon by his wife as honest and trustworthy.
- The husband had never said that he was unhappy in the marriage or thinking of leaving, and the wife believed herself to be in a secure relationship.
- The husband typically blurts out the news that the marriage is over "out of the blue" in the middle of a mundane domestic conversation.
- Reasons given for his decision are nonsensical, exaggerated, trivial or fraudulent.
- By the time the husband reveals his intentions to his wife, the end of the marriage is already a fait accompli and he often moves out quickly.

- The husband's behavior changes radically, so much so that it seems to his wife that he has become a cruel and vindictive stranger.

- The husband shows no remorse; rather, he blames his wife and may describe himself as the victim.

- In almost all cases, the husband had been having an affair.

- The husband makes no attempt to help his wife, either financially or emotionally, as if all positive regard for her has been completely extinguished.

- Systematically devaluing the marriage, the husband denies what he had previously described as positive aspects of the couple's joint history.

ACTION ITEMS:

☐ Write your story. Just do It! All of it … Yell, scream, cry, and keep writing. It's important and cathartic.

☐ Write letters to yourself to remind you to be strong… you've got this.

☐ Make lists of the things you need to accomplish, remember, or do

☐ PERSONAL SUGGESTION: Start working with a therapist who is schooled in trauma. It is worth the time if you are out a few months from the discard as the first few months are a blur.

CHAPTER 3

THE DISCARD

Journal
November 22, 2022
(1 month after Discard)

I hate you, Matthew. I cannot believe that you, of all people, chose to hurt me like this. You are mean and insane. You have been horrible to me, and I thought that it was your health—and to find that you have been plotting this for years and stringing me along. Slut/Cunt, this was what you called me when mad, and I forgave you, but you really hated me. I think I was beginning to see it. You want a separation for two years, and then I'm gone? Where am I going, or where are you going? I got a lawyer, and I am going to build my life in a way so you can never hurt me again. You are a sick man.

How did I not know I was married to a covert narcissist for 31 years?

Go ahead and google it... the answers are generic and ridiculous. Google "What is a covert narcissist?"

Whew! Right, and this is where the need for this book comes in...
you can find way too many different answers and no solutions.

I will suggest that you checkout *15 Signs of a Clinically Covert
Narcissist Husband* (marriage.com).

LET ME INTRODUCE YOU TO THE LINGO AND PATTERNS:

- IDEALIZATION: when the relationship is new you are the center of their world, they will be likable and call and have everything in common with you doing everything to win you over. This is love bombing, and it is hard to see when you are in it but the purpose is to get you addicted to their attention.

- DEVALUATION: now that you are in and usually married or pregnant, the narcissist will change the treatment toward you. They will be mad and then happy, become overly critical and compare you to others, give you the silent treatment, and then apologize.

- GASLIGHTING: (you are the problem) and this is the worst part of the treatment because it shakes our reality and we cannot believe what we think and see anymore. They activate you and then blame you for any reaction, thus creating shame.

- TRIANGULATION: intentionally makes you jealous. They treat you in an underhanded way and treat others wonderfully. They bring someone else into the relationship, a relative, an ex-mistress, in my case, many work wives, and a high school sweetheart. His last work wife in Montana, Jessica, told me at a company function that my husband does not want to live on Staten Island so don't do my home searching there. That was a fight, and it is sick that they thrive on this.

- TURNING OTHERS AGAINST YOU: During a divorce, prepare for a smear campaign where you will become the crazy person they are escaping from. They have no emotions and can transform into whomever they are talking to. I always thought everyone liked my husband, but the fact is that he was just playing them and if it went deeper, he could not have friends. They have a herd of codependents, other narcissists, empaths, and people pleasers and can easily turn all against you.

- HIDING THEIR TRUE SELF: they only present traits and qualities that they want seen and can disguise themselves. This is hard to spot in the beginning. You will see yourself as the problem in the relationship as the there is no empathy in the treatment you are receiving.

Then, The Discard... you ask yourself, *what did I do?*

You saw the mask slip or showed up strong and they resent your strength. This is the instant war you were not prepared for, but they planned all along. They have calculated their every move and anticipated your every response and you will witness the contemptuous abusive person who was there all along but has never felt anything for you.

For us, this war starts with the Discard. Yes, you are in a war, but you may have been shocked that the person you love and trusted the most always planned to do this to you. Specialists try to take the sting out of it and say, "You were nothing special. No matter what they said, they were only using you for their needs and this would always have ended this way." I could not believe it at first, but now, two years after the discard, I realize I have no idea who I was married to for 31 years.

In the book *Narcissistic Abuse and Codependency* by Courtney Evans, she explains what a relationship is like for us empathic codependents.

> *"Being in love with a narcissist is more like being in a prison. They use different tricks and strategies to manipulate you. They discover the qualities that make us human-like, compassion, love and sentimentality and use them against you. It is true partners of narcissists tend to feel betrayed that the romantic person they fell in love with disappeared over time (and fed you BREADCRUMBS like a nice written birthday card). It is disturbing and one will have numerous questions as to what they did wrong or what they failed to do to make the person disappear... this is intended from the beginning."*

Our focus on the covert narcissist in this chapter is much more than what happened but how we need to begin to recover. I have recommended books and links to educate yourself. Still, once you know that's enough to see what happened and to be aware of how you need to **Retreat and Protect** yourself from these characters in your life. Yes, they can be friends, lovers, parents, and children, and boy, will you notice you have a whole group of them and once discovered, expect most of these relations to fail... thankfully. From here let's educate and heal ourselves from it and help others devastated by this unknown silent abuse.

The first divorce book I read after my discard was *Runaway Husbands* by Vikki Stark. I began to piece together the mysterious end of my marriage. Stark is a therapist whose story is similar to ours. She developed a list of attributes that most of us share.

Hallmarks of Wife Abandonment Syndrome

by Vikki Stark author of *Runaway Husbands*

Do you suspect that you're a victim of Wife Abandonment Syndrome? Here are the ten defining characteristics that will let you know if you are. You don't need to check off all ten to fit the definition.

1. Before the separation, the husband seemed to be an attentive, emotionally engaged spouse, and his wife looked upon him as honest and trustworthy.

2. The husband never said that he was unhappy in the marriage or thinking of leaving, and the wife believed herself to be in a secure relationship.

3. The husband typically announces that the marriage is over "out of the blue" during a mundane domestic conversation.

4. The reasons given for his decision are nonsensical, exaggerated, trivial, or fraudulent.

5. By the time the husband reveals his intentions to his wife, the end of the marriage is already a fait accompli, and he often moves out quickly.

6. The husband's behavior changes radically, so much so that it seems to his wife that he has become a cruel and vindictive stranger.

7. The husband shows no remorse; instead, he blames his wife and may describe himself as the victim.

8. In almost all cases, the husband had been having an affair.

9. The husband makes no attempt to help his wife, either financially or emotionally, as if all positive regard for her has been completely extinguished.

10. Systematically devaluing the marriage, the husband denies what he had previously described as positive aspects of the couple's joint history."

I had checked off eight items when I attended Vikki's seminar three months after my discard and later found out about the affair partner, experienced financial and emotional attacks throughout the court and divorce proceedings, and saw our whole life rewritten from a completely different perspective.

Having learned something along my healing journey that is so hard to comprehend is that they always planned to do this to you. You were future-faked into believing that you had a future, and that they were forever committed to the relationship and you. You were used as domestic labor, daycare, sex, and in many other ways. That supply can be accessed from us because they need to fill their empty life.

I lived for years focusing on my spouse's career because he ended up in an industry that, as a white man, would allow him to rise to the top. So, we relocated, missed family, and spent holidays and birthdays without them. I spent my life ensuring everything at home was calm and under control, clean with dinner on the table when he and my daughter were able to come home. I sacrificed my career to part-time jobs and more relocations until he reached a level higher than our wildest dreams, and then the *Discard* came.

I am not trying to play the victim card. I was entirely on board with the plans we decided on and our future savings, but I was not aware that there would be a discard. If I had known the game I was in, I would have had a choice to participate or not, but that is the curiousness of it all... you would never know because if you did, you would not stay.

But we need to realize that once we find out we are in a relationship with a covert, we need to evaluate ourselves, heal, and correct what we are and what we got from that relationship. We need to take responsibility for ourselves, and this is where your healing will begin.

Initially, I was told by my husband we did not need lawyers and we would be divorced in two years. He would date, and we would still be best friends. He would pay my house bills, but I would walk away with nothing. At 57, I was expected to re-enter the workforce and earn enough to support myself. He would walk with our six-million dollar estate and force me out of the last home we had that I spent three years preparing for our retirement. Then, in court, he lied about everything he could lie about, not caring about being under oath and skillfully switching one word to skew the truth. It was shocking. He testified that I could have worked and contributed to the family; I did, but not at his level.

I was unaware that the statistics were in favor of this happening to me.

"A new analysis of divorce data from 1990 to 2021, released in July by Bowling Green State University's National Center for Family and Marriage Research found that divorce rates for those age 45 and over rose during that period, while rates dropped for those younger than 45. The most significant increase in divorce rates was among people 65 and older: The rate tripled from 1990 to 2021. At these older ages, rates of divorce among women nearly quadrupled. The phenomenon of older couples divorcing used to be rare. However, from

1990 to 2010, the rate doubled, according to Brown and Lin's analysis of U.S. Vital Statistics Reports from the Centers for Disease Control and Prevention and American Community Survey data from the U.S. Census Bureau.

"By 2010, twenty-seven percent of divorces were among those age 50 and older; by 2019, it grew to thirty-six percent. Digging into that data, the most recent available, Bowling Green researchers found that one in four divorces were among those age 65 or older."[1]

The reasons you find when googling WHY? are so common that most people I have talked to say none of them pertained to them: empty nest, financial problems, caring for aging parents, health issues, peer influence, getting married young, late-life abuse. I'm not saying none of this is true. Still, if you found yourself in "Sudden wife abandonment" and with a covert, you have been in an unknowing abusive relationship and need to heal from that specifically.

---

1   Study: Gray Divorce a Trend Among Boomers (aarp.org)

RESOURCES

BOOK/AUDIOBOOK:

- *The Covert Passive Aggressive Narcissist,* by Debbie Mirza. Recognizing the traits and finding healing after Hidden Emotional and Psychological Abuse. An essential book to help you "see the light" about your situation.

VOCABULARY:

LOVE BOMBING: is a form of psychological and emotional abuse that involves a person going above and beyond for you to manipulate you into a relationship with them. It looks different for every person, but it usually involves some form of excessive flattery and praise. Over-communication of their feelings for you. Showering you with unneeded/unwanted gifts. Early and intense talks about your future together.[2]

DOUBLE DISCARD: If you were discarded, chances are you were discarded previously and brought back in... Or if this is your first time being discarded, you will be brought back in again.[3]

---

2   What Is Love Bombing? 7 Signs To Look For (clevelandclinic. org) https://health.clevelandclinic.org/love-bombing#What%20 Is%20Love%20Bombing?

3   Narcissism, DEFINITION - Educational Journal of Narcissism. The narcissism network and centrality of narcissism features. - Document - Gale Health and Wellness

ACTION ITEMS:

☐ JOURNAL: Begin a daily gratitude Journal: Write 5 things that you are grateful for every day. I get cute notebooks from Dollar Tree, add a date and write 5 things no matter what, please:)

☐ EMPATHY SCALE: try this tool: As the empath, you will most likely answer high, and the narcissist will score low. Empathy Quotient (EQ) (psychology-tools.com)

CHAPTER 4

WHY ME? WHY YOU TOO?

Journal Entry

I am feeling so much shame and embarrassment in this smear campaign. It makes me feel inferior, humiliated, ashamed, embarrassed, and discouraged. I have started a chain of events that are not good for me... I am worrying about the future, Sad that I lost my friend, my best friend, and my father-in-law Gino, and the shame of failing in front of my family.

I need to remember that feelings are not the facts and that they are okay to have, but I cannot trust my mind. My mind is a wonderful servant but a terrible master.

I will call my friends and tell them my thoughts to get them out of my head. I need to remember how my higher power has been working in my life, and I have not been dropped on my butt yet.

It can be worse and I can do it that way with my thoughts. I can only control myself and not other people's opinions of me.

I had no idea how hated I was.

If your experience was anything like mine, you did not see this discard, separation, and divorce coming and you're knocked off your center. When this occurs, your mind begins to evaluate everything that has happened in your relationship. You look at every angle for an explanation because it all feels out of the blue and shocking. As noted in the Abandoned Wife Syndrome list, it comes out of nowhere.

Your mind will start to obsess and overwork, when you reach out to others. They will question you and offer their input. They may bring up other questions. Your mind will search for answers to those new questions you haven't thought of yet.

"Is he sick? Is there evidence of physical or mental illness?"

Initially, I could only allow myself to believe there was something wrong with him, and my love for him could not help.

This is where my (our) qualifier came into the picture. I had never heard of the term covert narcissist but surely I had heard codependent after working in therapy for years.

I want to caution you not to worry about labels or blame yourself. Chances are you have done that for years. This is only to shed light on how we heal. Our types of personalities are strong loving supportive people who would die for someone we love, and commitment means 100% commitment. That is how we are taken advantage of and I want you to join me in my healing journey so we can set healthy boundaries and see people that are harmful for who and what they are.

In The book *Groomed* by Elizabeth Melendez Fisher Good, the author points out that from birth we receive messages from "the secrets we keep, the messages we hear, and the stories we tell." We have no say in how we are programmed and who we become until we are aware and work on ourselves for ourselves.

Let's touch on a few personality traits that could describe people like us. This is a good topic for you to investigate to discover about yourself. We tend to want answers and focus on our partners, but I am asking that you change lanes, and I encourage you to consider what elements in the list below describe you. Be honest with yourself I promise that later in this book we will use this knowledge for your healing.

Are you a:

- codependent,
- people-pleaser,
- empath,
- caretaker,
- or a combination of all or some of the above?

It's okay if this describes you, but let's explore and try to bring attention to our personality characteristics and become healthier people for our future selves.

1. Codependents have a loss of self. This is different from the behavior of a covert narcissist who hides themselves. In reality, both have had some form of trauma in childhood and in this match, each looks to fulfill themselves and address that trauma with the other partner. The one difference is the codependent fills a need and the covert fills a plan.

2. People-pleasers, like codependents and coverts, probably had messages from adults that they could not deal with the child's feelings. The people-pleaser learns to see other people's wants and needs as more important than their own and goes out of their way to help others. Therefore, they can be exploited easily by others.

3. Empaths are highly sensitive people and their relationship with the covert is very parasitic. The covert narcissist will take all they can from empath who then and may never receive the award of love they are working so hard for.

None of us got out of childhood unharmed. This book is written mainly for those in a gray divorce so you are likely of a certain age. It would seem that a part of the problem is that in the 60s and 70s, we were not discussing these things and we certainly were not healing from them. Words like ADD and ADHD were not common until the mid-90s. Mental health and healing in the U.S. is a recent topic. Add to the fact that we were mostly latchkey kids and many of us were raised by hippies and men returning from Vietnam. We have some issues to heal.

Growing up in the 1970s in the northeast, I had two workaholic parents and was a latchkey kid. I learned to cook for myself and could fry eggs and bake cookies by the time I was in 1st grade. My grandmother's house is where I spent most weekends and summers. She too was codependent, and my grandfather was an alcoholic. Even as a kid, I saw that we needed to do whatever we had to in order to keep the marriage and family happy no matter how we were treated. My grandmother's religion taught her that it was her duty to sacrifice and she would be blessed no matter what. I see myself in her when I have perfectionistic bouts and go above and beyond for others without holding my boundaries.

This was true in my dating experiences from the start. I liked someone who liked me because I had a low sense of self-being and was operating from fear as a codependent empath. It's hard to be yourself because you don't know who you are... the word martyr comes to mind. I have always just blended into my family, relationships, and work. I could never say no, and that caused me a lot of anxiety and stress. That led to counseling and therapy to help me focus on surviving my daily life.

In *The Codependents Guide to the 12 Steps*, author Melody Beattie states something I can relate to. "I thought I was doing everything right. Aren't people supposed to be perfect? I'm stoic. Keep pushing forward no matter how much it hurts. Give until it hurts."

I am an empath with codependency attributes. My therapists all told me in my situation with my husband and daughter that I had to "retreat and protect myself." I was not told to leave the marriage or dangerous situation or seek other help outside of helping myself, ever, not even one time.

> *"Empaths can have codependent tendencies, but not all codependents are empaths. The difference is that empaths absorb the stress, emotions, and physical symptoms of others, something not all codependents do."*[4]

I can feel your feelings from a state away. I know what you are feeling when something happens to you and will take that on myself and experience that as an empath. If you were unknowingly a victim of a covert narcissist, I am so sorry. It is heartbreaking to see that so many of us had no idea what we were a part of and how we were controlled, minute by minute, by masterful manipulations. They always planned to discard us in the most painful way possible.

Another reason it is hard to comprehend and heal from this is that there are a lot of medical studies showing that they have proven if you have been exposed to long-term covert abuse from a narcissist, you have experienced brain damage. It is painful to reflect on that and it took a year before I could see and understand that and realize my husband's part and mine in what was

---

4   From *The Difference Between Being an Empath & a Codependent* (drjudithorloff.com)

happening. The following is from a published article on Hack Spirit, truly a great reliable resource for self-improvement.

> *"There is also a physical aspect of brain damage involved— when suffering consistent emotional abuse, victims experience a shrinking of the hippocampus and a swelling of the amygdala; both of these circumstances lead to devastating effects. The hippocampus is crucial in learning and developing memories, while the amygdala is where negative emotions like shame, guilt, fear, and envy come to life... But the first step is ultimately the most important one: getting out of the destructive and abusive relationship. Before any progress can be made towards recovery, the victim must acknowledge the situation and accept his or her reality... This type of abuse isn't just about anger or other emotions; rather, it's about power. This abuse can manifest at the physical, spiritual, emotional, mental, financial, and even sexual levels. And in many cases, the victim isn't even fully aware of the abusive dynamic of their relationship... This is because narcissists understand the art of manipulation more than most, and can convince even the most abused partners that the fault of every fight is on their hands."* [5]

As I wrote this book, I was 17 months into a contentious divorce and my eyes became open, but because of our age, most information I came across on the internet and some books I've read are geared toward young families with children and not as applicable to my situation. Perhaps you can relate. Therapy, reading, and research have led me to what I feel is the beginning of a wonderful life and I hope to help you too.

---

5   *Neuroscience: The shocking impact narcissistic abuse has on the brain* - Hack Spirit

A Letter From Matt
January 2023
(Just three months after discard... you will not hear the
dog whistles, but I do. He wanted to hurt me and cancel
the divorce.)

I hope this letter finds you well. I think you are well aware of my handwriting, as such I am typing this letter. I felt the need to reach out. I know this has been difficult for both of us, but I truly hope you are doing well. I don't want you to hate me, but that is probably me being selfish. I want you to know I really care about you, and I carry much guilt for separating and how abruptly it was done.

When you and Carly dropped me off at the airport, I did not know it would be the last time we would all be together (dog whistle he planned it).

I need to explain myself so you know the truth, MY truth.

I did not plan this at all, and I certainly did not trick you, get involved with someone else *[bought a home for another woman three months after this letter]*, or wait for that opportunity.

I have been having a really hard time emotionally particularly while you were going to Florida *[he sent me to furnish our retirement home]* and I would have time by myself and question if I missed you or if I was just sad with our relationship and my personal life was not bad but I found it unfulfilling, so I would become disconnected and disengaged, but I also don't know that I have ever been able to give myself 100 percent to you or to the relationship, and I don't know why. I really did try.

Then I came to realize this was a cycle I had been going through, and even though I would work on being married and trying to make it feel fulfilling for you and me it was only temporary.

I don't think there is anything that you could have done differently. I care about you, but I did not realize that I was not in love.

You might be in a completely different space than me on all of this your perspective is your own, and I respect that, but I felt the need to tell you about my struggle.

I don't know what I'm expecting from this letter. Maybe it will help me?

I definitely did not send it to you to hurt you, but you needed to hear my side and know this is about me and what I'm dealing with. You know I don't talk to anyone about this stuff *[warning about future smear campaigns]*, and it doesn't help that I'm unable to talk to you about it because I get really upset. If you're angry with me, I will not bother you again and we will just let the legal stuff wrap up. I'm still hopeful there will be a time when we are friends (future faking).

Matt

[During our Divorce trial a year later, all this was a different story.]

I meet at least one person a day who has gone through the sudden end of a relationship, and most times they have never discussed the discard with anyone and thought it was just them that this has happened to. Last week, at the dog park, I met Maria who has been divorced for 23 years and had this experience and it affected her so much that she never remarried. I met a woman whose husband cashed out their business and invested poorly and incorrectly days before he discarded her. At age 65, the money was gone and they had owned an 11-million-dollar business. Just imagine going from tremendous prosperity to nothing overnight. I am in the same boat.

My husband has been stockpiling large amounts of money away for years and told the judge, "I don't want her to have it because she did not earn it." Look I am not even trying to split our estate 50/50, far less. It is below that but that does not make him happy although that was initially his proposal. This also fueled my desire to write a Divorce Resource to navigate the Family Court system through your divorce and in that, we will address suggestions to guide you through your divorce.

RESOURCES

BOOKS:

- *Narcissistic Abuse and Codependency,* by Courtney Evans
- *Healing from Hidden Abuse: A Journey Through the Stages of Recovery from Psychological Abuse,* by Shannon Thomas, LLCs'

VOCABULARY:

DOG WHISTLE: Have you ever experienced abuse where you were the only one who knew it was abuse? You may have experienced "dog whistling," a covert form of abuse that is intended to strategically disorient the victim while escaping accountability. In the context of abusive relationships, dog-whistling can be used to target and terrorize the victim. Narcissistic and psychopathic individuals can use insidious and diverse forms of dog whistling to covertly manipulate and belittle their victims while escaping consequences, accountability, and judgment from others. [6]

ACTION ITEMS:

- ☐ WATCH THIS: Ramani on YouTube "What does it mean to go "no contact"?
- ☐ AND THIS: Med Circle on YouTube "Narcissist Abuse | The Signs"

---

6   *How Narcissists Use 'Dog Whistling' To Covertly Abuse You,* by Thought Catalog

CHAPTER 5

THE COVERT NARCISSIST

Covert Narcissism:

> *"Covert narcissism (also known as vulnerable narcissism) is the more introverted side of NPD (narcissism personality disorder). A covert narcissist experiences the same insecurities as an overt narcissist, but internalizes their self-importance, often while hyper-focusing on their need for attention...Covert narcissists, though, are people who fly under the radar. Even if you've been in a relationship with someone for years, their covert narcissism may be so subtle that you're not even aware of it for a very long time. That's what makes covert narcissism a little more dangerous and a little more difficult to manage. Take the way we respond to anger, for example. Where an overt narcissist might be very expressive with their rage in outward, obvious, aggressive ways, a covert narcissist may direct their anger inward by becoming self-deprecating or by participating in passive-aggressive behavior. In some cases, a covert narcissist may even be better at revenge because they keep their true feelings hidden by suppressing them...Covert narcissists don't feel like they're doing anything wrong."* [7]

---

[7] Definition from CleavlandClinic.org

When was the first time you heard this term? I had never heard of this previously but it explains what happened to me to a tee. I was called a narcissist by my daughter, and insecure and jealous by my husband. But I did not know why and how that groomed me into what they needed me to be.

Journal Entry
October 22, 2012
(First Al-anon in-person meeting)

I cried and went back to a room with a woman. My husband is trying to hurt me and is constantly on me about my weight, withholding sex, looking at other women and lying all the time. All so passive-aggressive and it seems that the next step will be him cheating on me. I try to complete him and help him and enable him to have a good career, and love him, and he resents it. He is completely detached, and I don't know how to handle this anymore. I deserve better than someone who cannot be themselves with me. Someone who knows they would not cheat or do something to hurt me. Someone who appreciates me.

Journal Entry
October 25, 2012

I had a conversation with Matt at dinner last night and he reassured me that we are working on things and then he looked weirdly excited and said, "Unless that's not what you want?" That was a kick in my chest and it felt like the prospect of me wanting out of the marriage would give him some kind of break. I am hurt and cannot let it go, and he just yells at me telling me I am crazy. He keeps doing the same thing, taking calls during sex to stop, not listening to me, and yelling at me. I am sick and sensitive and need to focus on me.

Journal Entry
October 26, 2012

Horror, Matt left, Hurricane Sandy hit our town, I have pneumonia, we got an early snowstorm, no work, no electricity, no TV and no cell service, and no heat.

Journal Entry
November 8, 2012

The grief and pain are killing me and I want to die. I need to realize that I don't have to accept unacceptable behavior, but I never experience acceptable behavior from anyone in my home and they say it's all my fault... I don't know where his sexual needs are being met, he does not like my body and is having an emotional affair at work. I feel empty, alone, and unloved. I feel his anger and just wait for the explosion. I am being manipulated and my daughter told me I have never made them happy and they hate me. I hate this fucking triangle between me, Matthew, and Sara. It has always been a problem. I am married to an ADD workaholic in a mid-life crisis with a constant mistress.

Journal Entry
December 2, 2012

Feeling disconnected with Matthew. He is with someone else and said I need to work on myself. He screamed at me that he is sick of me and Sara, and it should be about him right now. I listen to him talk about his future and no plans include me...

What I am hearing:

Matthew -your insecurities have led to your unhappiness.

Sara- You have never been happy with Dad.

My Heart- I am not happy and I am afraid.

Family- all think we are getting a divorce.

Matthew keeps saying, "It will all be okay and there is no easy way to end our marriage."

Months.... Years.... Decades. I wish I had ended my marriage then, but we went on for 10 more years.

"Living with or being involved with a narcissist can be mentally and emotionally exhausting. It can feel like you have to perform "mental gymnastics" from dealing with the lying (even when confronted with undeniable proof), the gaslighting, the triangulation, the projection, the constant contradictions, the manipulation, blame-shifting, the charm they lay on, the inflated sense of self - even subtle forms of torture, such as sleep-deprivation these people inflict on their victims - appears to be conscious and calculated to push the target of their "affections" past their limits, into surrender - and ultimately into total compliance - as a source of Narcissistic Supply. Children, spouses, friends, and lovers - those closest to the Narcissist - are not considered individuals in their own right by the Narcissist - but rather extensions or, in the worst

cases, the property of the Narcissist... if you don't protect or remove yourself from the situation, you may find yourself entering into a state of mind where you instinctively try to fix or fight the narcissist's illogical attitudes and behaviors. You may find yourself becoming hyper-vigilant, trying to second guess them, trip them up, lay down ultimatums, call them on their lies, or constantly trying to stay one step ahead of their ever-changing rulebook. Narcissists are like psychological vampires, attaching themselves to you in a way that drains you of your resources (emotional, mental, and financial) and leaves you questioning your worth and sanity. Often, narcissists can imitate or approximate caring about others when it is convenient for them to do so. However, they typically do not perceive that anything outside of their sphere of wants and needs matters. It simply doesn't occur to them to consider the needs of anyone else or the long-term consequences of their behaviors. Narcissists can be highly intelligent, witty, talented, likable, and fun to be around. They can also elicit sympathy like nobody's business. Narcissists are opportunistic. They can make a show of being "generous" but their generosity usually has strings attached. They tend to isolate their victims, sucking up their time and energy, many times robbing their own families, spouses, and partners of an external support system. Narcissists are excellent liars and many prefer to lie, even when telling the truth would be more beneficial to them. They are often highly competitive and argumentative. They can be calculating and extremely persuasive and susceptible to erratic thinking and impulsive decision-making. narcissism is commonly co-morbid with addictions to drugs, alcohol, sex, food, spending, and gambling. It has been suggested that narcissists have a higher rate of ADHD than the general population. Narcissists are rarely alone. They like to feed on the energy of others, and to have an audience to reflect back to them the person they want to see themselves as... typically do not feel compassion or empathy or consider the feelings or well-being of others.

They tend to be singularly focused on getting their own needs met, at the expense of the needs of others. While narcissists generally portray a lack of conscience, they typically have an intellectual awareness of what they are doing and how they hurt others. They simply do not care."[8]

The Covert Passive Aggressive Narcissist by Debi Mizra will help you immediately see the relationship dynamics, and determine if this was the relationship you experienced and all the hows and whys you have been asking yourself. The last chapter addresses healing and how we prevent this from happening to us again. This is a great resource I have recommended in multiple support groups and the response from others is that it's very helpful.

I promised myself that I would heal, read every book, attend every seminar, and listen to every podcast so that I would not be in this situation again, but funny enough, that is the same determination I used to stay and work on my marriage for years. The difference was allowing the chains to slip and focus on myself. Is it easy to do? NO! Is it worth it? Yes! It's only you and you are the only one who can and will do this for you. I will share as many of the resources I have found that all combined have led me to a good place one year after the discard but remember you are not in a bubble of healing... life still happens, and the divorce will be the worst thing you have ever experienced in life, but you can heal and learn to focus on you today and relying on your spiritual laurels (we will talk about this later but I developed a new relationship with a higher power and it is so important to have this to survive).

To know and educate yourself is to protect your future self.

---

8   *Out of the Fog,* by Dana Mornningstar

Where classic narcissists are wolves in wolves' clothing, covert narcissists are wolves in sheep's clothing. They may appear unassuming or even shy, but underneath lies the same self-absorption, need for control, and lack of empathy that defines all narcissistic personality disorders.[9]

9   https://medium.com/psychology-simplified/
    covert-narcissists-wolves-in-sheeps-clothing-e839188eb35

RESOURCES

BOOKS/ AUDIOBOOKS

- *In Sheep's Clothing: Understanding and Dealing with Manipulative People,* by George K. Simon Jr Ph.D.
- *Start Here: A Crash Course in Understanding, navigating and healing from Narcissist Abuse,* by Dana Morningstar

VOCABULARY:

DARVO: Deny, Attack and Reverse Victim and Offender
"Used to deflect responsibility onto an individual they abused and is a form of manipulation. Deny what you have witnessed attacking you with names or tell you your jealous insecure etc." [10]

RULE OF THREE: the stages of covert relationships Idealize, Devalue, and Discard.

COVERT NARCISSISM: "Covert narcissism (also known as vulnerable narcissism) is the more introverted side of NPD (narcissism personality Disorder). A covert narcissist experiences the same insecurities as an overt narcissist, but internalizes their self-importance, often while hyper-focusing on their need for attention...Covert narcissists, though, are people who fly under the radar. Even if you've been in a relationship with someone for years, their covert narcissism may be so subtle that you're not even aware of it for a very long time. That's what makes covert narcissism a little more dangerous and a little more difficult to manage. Take the way we respond to anger, for example. Where

---

10 medicalnewtoday.com

an overt narcissist might be very expressive with their rage in outward, obvious, aggressive ways, a covert narcissist may direct their anger inward by becoming self-deprecating or by participating in passive-aggressive behavior. In some cases, a covert narcissist may even be better at revenge because they keep their true feelings hidden by suppressing them...Covert narcissists don't feel like they're doing anything wrong."[11]

---

11   ClevelandClinic.org

WILL THE DEATH OF US BE THE DEATH OF ME?

CHAPTER 6

HEALING

"Someday, we'll forget the hurt, the reason we cried and who caused us the pain. We will finally realize that the secret of being free is not revenge, but letting things unfold in their own way and own time. After all, what matters is not the first, but the last chapter of our life which shows how well we ran the race. So, smile, laugh, forgive, believe, and love all over again." [12]

I added this into my journal 12 years before my divorce. I was hurting then and this is what we are here for now, **The Healing**, and why I feel the need to write this book. So many of the hundreds of people who join Narcissist Abuse support groups online daily all seem to have the same questions at the beginning of the discovery of the situation or after the discard. Then, we all begin the search for answers and refer to books, internet searches, and TikTok. I find that people are coming to the groups for answers but need to take the responsibility to educate themselves.

One member told us that she is still angry, shocked, and broken. She decided her husband may come back if she were sick and has laid in bed for two years after the discard. When her ex-husband

---

12 midlifegroup.com

drops off their teens after school, she is mad because he does not check on her. This may just seem like her trying to manipulate him but it's a victim's reaction to the abuse she suffered previously.

At the beginning of my divorce, another woman posted in a support group, "I am 10 years out and cannot stop ruminating and still love him and want him back even knowing I was in an abusive relationship. I will wait and try until I die."

I did not want to experience either of these things in my life even though, at first, I thought I could and felt blessed to read such disheartening responses. It made me determined not to dwell in the abuse and recover.

But you do dwell and that is a healthy part of recovery from covert abuse. We ruminate while our mind searches for answers and explanations, and I can see my mind sorting and filing all past life events with my husband and daughter with the information that I have to now define and make sense of. The more you learn, the more you will begin to ruminate or, as I call it, connect the dots to see what happened. It's hard, but if you go through it, preferably with a trained professional, it will get better.

You need to first realize that this is abuse and that you are in an abusive relationship. It's very hard to come to terms with and admit to ourselves, let alone to others in our life. Therapy with an abuse recovery and divorce specialist has been beneficial for me and I went weekly for the first year after my discard. I have found two medications with my primary and psychiatrist that have helped me mentally and emotionally and have healed the health concerns the sudden discard caused. I want to share this with you because like the lady above we cannot waste 10 years of our lives stuck. We, now more than ever, need to heal to help the army of others who are escaping this life of secret abuse.

Let me explain to you what the discard did to me. Before my discard, I had rheumatoid arthritis which flared up when my husband left me the first time and it almost crippled me. I became a vegetarian for years to heal that and it finally went into remission. A few years before my discard, I was gaslighted by my husband and my adult daughter that she was not my husband's child. That threw me into trauma because I had never slept with anyone else and she was clearly his child. He was suggesting that I slept around or cheated on him, which was blatantly untrue, and he refused to take a paternity test. This started me to have some mental problems, stress, and disconnect from reality. I started to believe that I got killed in a car accident with my dog on my way home to see my husband and that could be the only reason to explain what was going on in my life. I was losing my mind trying to understand why they would want to hurt me this way. My mind was trying to find a way to make sense of it even if it meant I created an alternate reality in my head.

My husband wanted me to lose weight, which then, of course, did not allow me to lose weight because I wasn't losing weight for myself and I felt that I was disappointing him again. After the second discard, my kidney functions dropped into the single digits. I became a prediabetic, my rheumatoid arthritis flared up, and I had severe depression all within one week of being discarded. I was told by my doctor that I needed to go get sexual disease tests done because most likely my husband was having an affair. I had to go to a clinic and get STD testing. I recommend this for everyone if you think that your husband has been cheating.

This is the point where I realized what I was witnessing with other people who could not get over their discard from their covert narcissist. My health was failing and I needed to put myself first to survive and heal. As older people, we have the benefit of having close relationships and no children in the home, so we can take time to do the work to recover. This would be the first time in my life I needed to choose to put myself first and become, dare I say, selfish.

I had to learn about the relationship I was in and I hope you can read the books suggested because it is the only way to understand that if you were not in a normal relationship, this is what has happened to you. You have to accept that you are not special to them, except for supply, that they never loved you, no matter what they said, that you never knew them, and the person they are now you do not know. It's gut-wrenching to think this and harder to believe it. Family and friends will not want to or cannot believe it themselves.

In the book *Healing from Hidden Abuse* by Shannon Thomas, LCSW on page 173 she added a letter for family and friends to read to help understand our experience and support us. Let me share a piece here:

Dear Family and Friends Your Loved One Isn't Crazy

"...Your loved one met someone who they had fully and truly fallen in love with and wanted to spend the rest of their lives loving. Your loved one was authentic in his or her feelings toward the other person. However, your loved one met a con artist. They pretended to have feelings for your loved one and strategically set up the whole entire relationship to meet her or his own abusive needs.

"Toxic people derive great entertainment from taking a healthy and happy person like your loved one and completely ruining their life. Hard to imagine, right? As a therapist, I can tell you it's 100% true. Your loved one may have tried to share this information with you but it was hard for you to believe. You may have even liked the toxic person. Guess what? You were scammed too, drawing in family and friends as part of the staged affection the toxic person exhibited is done to gain your trust that they are a good honest person. How does this work to their advantage when your loved one comes and tells you the nasty and horrible things that happen to them? You question them and their perspective. Maybe you even knowingly side with the toxic person against your loved one.

"In reality, many survivors of psychological abuse develop post-traumatic stress disorder (PTSD). There are triggers that bring on intense anxiety and times of the year that will be harder than others for your loved ones. Normal sad, but if it's normal, why does the abuse cause trauma and a long recovery? Your loved one experienced systematic and repeated covert psychological abuse. The toxic person set out to destroy your loved one. No matter how nice he or she presents themself to you, listen to what your loved one tells you about the true character of this person. Really listen. Above all, believe your loved one when they confide in you that they were abused. Forgive yourself for not noticing the abuse. Come together with your loved one to move forward. Basically, the person wanted to destroy your loved one and all of his or her relationships. Please do not let this plan succeed. Issue all the best as you support your loved one in their recovery. I truly believe that our days are ahead for you both."

Let's move even deeper into our recovery!

RESOURCES

VOCABULARY

RUMINATING: constant replay and thinking about specific situations. Result of covert abuse.

COVERT: *"The word covert means anything that is hidden or less outright or obvious and so, in terms of abuse, convert abuse is abuse that is often hidden, less outright or obvious. Some more common examples of covert abuse would be emotional or psychological abuse or subtle forms of verbal abuse even physical abuse that doesn't leave a large mark.*

Some covert abuse is abuse that goes unnoticed. More common examples of covert abuse would be emotional or psychological abuse or subtle forms of verbal abuse even physical abuse that doesn't leave a large mark can be viewed as covert. To fly under the radar of most people might be name calling, teasing, sarcasm, being brutally honest, minimizing or denying a person's reality or experience also known as gaslighting especially if they speak up and have a problem with how they're being treated. The abuser might say things such like that never happened, you are crazy or spinning things back around and blaming them for misremembering, baiting a person into a circular conversation that is designed to show an intellectual superiority and humiliating a person, frustrating them, grinding them down, exhausting them or provoking your reaction, so that the narcissist can point at them and exclaim how abusive and manipulative their partner really is. Physical abuse can also be done in covert ways such as pinching, spitting, shoving, slapping or even hitting or leaving bruises in areas that will be covered by clothing...

A note on overt... the word overt means anything that is outright or obvious and for many people overt abuse is anything that

is usually physical abuse that leaves physical marks such as a
bruises or broken bones or intense verbal and emotional reviews
or yelling or belittling is involved."[13]

PETITIONER: The person who makes a formal application to the
court for divorce.

RESPONDENT: The position of the defendant in a lawsuit

NO-FAULT DIVORCE: Divorce that requires no wrongdoing to
be granted

AT FAULT DIVORCE: Divorce that needs proof of wrongdoing.

COURT-ASSISTED FINANCIAL ABUSE: A person using the court
system to control and financially wound the victim.

---

13 *Out of the Fog*, Y Dana Morningstar

WILL THE DEATH OF US BE THE DEATH OF ME?

CHAPTER 7

FROM BROKEN FAIRYTALES
TO DIVORCE REALITIES

So, you have been discarded or finally left your covert relationship... you are out!

If your experience is anything like the ending of my relationship, it came suddenly, unexpectedly, and with a long list of rules from my husband. Just before the discard I was tricked into selling my home under the guise we were relocating, but he had to get rid of that home to buy his mistress a home in New Jersey.

The list included: no lawyers, no divorce for two years, he will date, I can stay in our Florida home, he will continue to pay the home bill for two years, end all TV subscriptions, and stop payment to World Hunger Program (we supported for 25 years). The daily emails and texts would not stop and my friend and I started to call the multiple daily emails with financial demands his "money porn." It seemed he was getting off on cutting me off. If I protested, he would say, "I'm sorry this is complicated," and then send another demand. I was flabbergasted and started to reach out to lawyers in Montana because it would take me six months to become a resident of Florida and I had a weird feeling that this was heading south very quickly. At this point, I did not know of the affair or of all the money that had been accumulated and hidden for years under the excuse that it was for our retirement and other bill payment accounts. So much money and more to be discovered later.

The company my husband works for is the top employer in Montana, and I could not find a lawyer that did not have a conflict of interest except one and that is who I went with to file to stop my husband from draining all our accounts. Thankfully, I did because in plain sight during the divorce he prepaid 50K to taxes only to get that as a return when he thought the marriage would have ended. I am 20 months into my divorce and the last trial was 10 months ago with no final decree issued, yet more money was found, another motion was filed and possibly another court date to be set.

My husband's story is that he said he just wanted a separation and I suddenly filed for divorce. No mention of Beverly, his mistress, or all the other underhanded moves he made. For once in my life, I decided to protect myself, and boy, am I being attacked in every way you can imagine for that. This is where your healing needs to kick up. You will need to be stronger than you ever have in your life when you are divorcing a covert or just in a contentious divorce, they are brutal.

The problem here is the family court system is not geared to long-term, later-life, "gray" divorce. The courts are set up to focus on young families and children. When you bring in years of a stay-at-home mom and stay-at-home corporate wife, coupled with large retirements, pensions, and savings with homes and cars etc., it seems to fall apart. Most of the legal advice out there is geared toward the same audience. It's hard to find your way through the maze. I am going to share all the information that I found through months of research.

Please refer to your state and research all the state sites. Print out all the paperwork to read and highlight with questions for your lawyer interviews. Talk to as many lawyers as you can get on the phone. I will warn you to never mention the word narcissist because it is overused and does not apply without a diagnosis, which is hard if not impossible to get. Give examples of the experiences you are having. I had no idea that I was being financially abused and controlled until my lawyer and therapist brought this to my attention. My process experience has been in Montana, which is an equitable distribution, no-fault state. If you file first, you are the petitioner and they are the respondent. You will now go first with most things during the process, filing the discovery, mediation negotiations, and trial testimony. Had I known this, I would have worked with my lawyer to be more proactive in discovering what could be used against me and address the topic first, because although by Montana law they are a no-fault state, a covert will use the system to further abuse, control and humiliate you. Couple that with a narcissist lawyer and it is an abuse you will not forget; this has been my experience.

In the article, *It's Post-Separation Legal Abuse, Not High Conflict Divorce,* abusers torment their exes through the courts in a form of coercive control. From www.Psychologytoday.com, we see how we are abused in courts by our abusers also.

When abusers use the courts to harass their ex-partners, judges sometimes consider "the couple" as the problem, failing to identify the legal maneuvers as a form of continued abuse.

> *"... judges often mistakenly identify custody disputes involving a domestic abuser as "high conflict divorces." The term "high conflict divorce" suggests symmetrical and parallel escalation from both parties. However, in most "high conflict" divorce cases, what we are really seeing is one "party who is drawn towards, rather than away from, conflict" (Rosenfeld et al., 2019) ...These cases are marked by one "high conflict litigant" who exerts power by dragging their ex into court repeatedly. In other words, an abuser creates a*

series of court complications to make a divorce... impossible to resolve, so it continues for years. The problem is not the couple—the problem is one member of the couple and should be handled accordingly. The abuser wants the case to drag on, relishing these opportunities to continue to make the ex-partner suffer.

"This coercive control tactic is variously called legal abuse (Douglas, 2018), vexatious litigation (Fitch & Easteal, 2017), procedural abuse (Miller & Smolter, 2011), judicial terrorism (Tucker, 2021)... when their true goal is to maintain a continuous route for harassing their ex-partners.

"The abuser retains or regains control by bringing the victim back to court repeatedly. Each day in court takes a tremendous toll on the victim in lost wages and lawyer's fees. Victims of domestic abuse have often already suffered from financial abuse. The court battle may stretch them financially beyond the breaking point...Psychologically, the stress of prolonged court battles can be devastating to the protective parent and to the children."[14]

In my case, it's a reverse financial abuse tactic. As money is found, I need to go back to court and I look like an abuser, but I am not hiding or have access to large sums of money.

I will suggest a place to start is to run a credit report on yourself, get copies of all bank statements for a year if you have access, lock your credit, gather your mortgage paperwork, utility bills, and other bills, and get copies of last two years of tax returns, retirement paperwork for pensions, 401Ks, investment accounts and request a copy of their social security statement. Fill out budget planners and divorce forms to see where the money is and list where you might think there is more money. You will

---

14   Clements et al., 2021

need this information for your discovery and, hopefully, find other information from their discovery.[15]

It's overwhelming, but gather it all and go to a financial planner that will give you a free consultation. I had a bad experience with a divorce specialist financial planner and paid $3000 for 10 hours of nothing. Go to a free advisor. They will work until you get a settlement and you can decide if you want to work with them at that time. Your bank may also offer that but if you have joint accounts that could get confusing. Make the calls and ask questions, now is the time to become braver than you think you are, pretend to be a boss, and run your business, which is you!

The following website has a free resource (sign up) and good steps to get prepared for divorce: HelloDivorce.com (the Hello Divorce Worksheet)

---

15   Find FREE resources on my web page: https://graydivorcesupportgroup.com/resources/

RESOURCES

- **WEBSITE:** HelloDivorce.com (the Hello Divorce Worksheet). a free resource (sign up) Good steps to get prepared for divorce.

FINANCIAL RESOURCE IDEAS:

- **FORBES WEBSITE:** Divorce Checklist
- **EDWARD JONES:** Free Financial Consultation
- **WELLS FARGO:** Free Financial Consultations
- **CHASE:** Free Financial Consultations

BOOK/AUDIOBOOK:

- *Divorce Affirmations*, by Stephens Hyang
- *Will I ever be free of you?: How to navigate a high-conflict divorce from a narcissist and heal your family*, by Karyl McBride, PHD

VOCABULARY:

PETITIONER: the person who makes a formal application to the court for divorce.

RESPONDENT: The position of the defendant in a lawsuit

NO-FAULT DIVORCE: Divorce that requires no wrongdoing to be granted

AT FAULT DIVORCE: Divorce that needs proof of wrongdoing.

COURT-ASSISTED FINANCIAL ABUSE: A person using the court system to control and financially wound the victim.

CHAPTER 8

THE SMEAR CAMPAIGN

Journal Entry

I thought it was forever. I know my husband might not be someone else's taste but until the day it ended, I loved the way that he looked, his 6 foot 4 stature and his bald head. I never minded shaving his body for him. I felt that I fit perfectly under his armpit and that I belonged there.

He smelled like St. Ives moisturizer and Moroccan oil, which I got for him to use on his bald head. He liked Irish spring soap but the shower door clung to it.

I even miss his big floppy 13-inch feet, flat as a board with a scar down the instep.... the one that he cut open at Boy Scout camp one summer jumping off a dock.

I even loved the scratchy spot on his belly. Some days he would rub the scar on the top of my head, the one that I got at Christmas.

I thought I would be with him forever and ever. The things that were done to me I could never have imagined my worst enemy doing to me and they were done to me by the person who I loved the most. The accusations rip my heart out and the fact that he feels he is taking revenge on me kills me.

You will be shocked and hurt when you find out how much they hate you.

You will survive. It's not going to seem like you will, but you will. You need to begin your healing and focus on yourself, learning as much as you can as fast as you can so you will have some ground to hold onto when you experience this.

The smear campaign may come immediately or slowly as the separation and divorce proceedings develop. Most likely, it has already been going on for years with the supply. The other supply has already heard stories about how horrible, dumb, unfaithful, irresponsible, etc. you are. Whether they were a partner, work spouse, friend, your friends, there has always been an underlying allegiance forming with your spouse and others.

Have you ever noticed that they never defended you or always saw things from others' points of view? This was gaslighting and always meant to unbalance you.

Did you ever notice they always seemed to be someone else around others? During family gatherings, they are disengaged, sick, tired, and unable to help. During parties, they act like a college frat boy with the lampshade on their head by the end of the night. Any request you made for sobriety or assistance with a gathering was agreed to and then they somehow ruined it.

At their job, you may have been portrayed, just under the surface, as unreliable, a liar, etc. (don't worry this will be said in front of you on the stand to the judge, and you will wonder who your ex is talking about UNDER OATH).

After the initial discard call from my narcissist when he said, "I love you, but am not in love with you and I do not want to be married anymore," his story changed in two weeks as he started his new career in a new state without me. He told coworkers and friends, "She went to Florida and decided she did not want to come to New Jersey and then she served me divorce papers while at work." In his mind, this is somehow true and no matter what will be said, recorded, and written, he cannot believe anything other than the stories he tells himself. This is a typical pattern for the covert narcissist. They tell the lies so many times, to so many people, that they come to believe their own stories.

Have you hurt the narcissist? This holds a special place in their heart. You will go down in a slow burning death unlike any writer could write for a movie. It won't stop coming and you will be hoovered in with a nice email just before the next big attack... it is bizarre. Narcissists are always plotting and planning like a chess game. But if you ever hurt them, you are screwed. It's called the narcissistic injury. I never hurt my husband during our entire marriage but when that happens, the gloves come off and they will do anything to seek and exact revenge.

There are three stages of the Smear Campaign:[16]

1. The Lie

2. False Allegations

3. Smear Campaign

> *"Narcissists lie. You probably know that by now, but it's what they do to weaponize that lie to basically take you down, emotionally defending yourself, and financially defending yourself, and in court to prove your innocence against these false attacks. I believe we can remove the power we give them, but these lies affect us. Their goal with these is to certainly take you down simply because it's fun and they can, but also to make themselves the victim. The next step after the*

---

16 Narcissist Support.com

basic lie is to turn a lie into false allegations, which become the weapon. They often do this in every divorce case and the victim is left to defend their name, their honor, and the very thing that is their greatest strength. Then comes the smear campaign where they share these lies and false allegations with others and this can cause despair or panic when you hear these things." [17]

In the video with this article, Tracey Malone explains that the narcissist does not have a conscience, remorse, and empathy, so they cannot see that they have hurt you. The goal of this is for them to triangulate you, and to be seen as the hero, victim, or someone who tolerated you.

In therapy, I have learned that there is a power in letting go and not worrying about what others say and think about me. It's hard, but if people believe it, they never know the real you and we don't want to be the victim ourselves.

I called a trusted friend and let them know about the trauma lie I heard and asked to talk through it with me. We tried to prove to ourselves that this was a lie not to prove its truth. I wrote it in a journal to process it and discuss it with my therapist. It is a practice to let it go every time you are activated by these lies. The bottom line: Don't fall into self-blame and believe the lies. That is how we were ensnared for so long in the first place. Try with everything you have to pull yourself up and you will get stronger, I promise.

---

17 Three levels of smear campaigns and how to protect yourself - Narcissist Abuse Support

RESOURCES

BOOK/AUDIOBOOK:

- *Divorcing Your Narcissist: You Can't Make This Shit Up,* by Tracey Malone

TIKTOK :

- Lisa Lu - girl power real talk about the covert narcissist

VOCABULARY:

LIE: "The dictionary definition of lying is "to make a false statement with the intention to deceive" (OED 1989) ... the traditional definition of lying. ... there are at least four necessary conditions for lying. First, lying requires that a person make a statement (statement condition). Second, lying requires that the person believes the statement to be false; that is, lying requires that the statement be untruthful (untruthfulness condition). Third, lying requires that the untruthful statement be made to another person (addressee condition). Fourth, lying requires that the person intends that the other person believe the untruthful statement to be true (intention to deceive the addressee condition)."

WILL THE DEATH OF US BE THE DEATH OF ME?

CHAPTER 9

ADULT CHILDREN

Your children are most likely adults now. As someone in gray divorce, we most likely do not have younger children that we need to also manage and make plans for but that is not to say that it is not uncomfortable. Many of us have strained relationships with our children and find that they couldn't care less if they are in your life to care at all. During a gray divorce, adult children can have as many feelings and positions as there can be. Some are devastated by their image of their parents' marriage ending, some wonder how it lasted so long, and some are already in a fractured relationship with one or both parents that it does not seem to be in their universe. Add to this the covert narcissist piece of the puzzle and the whole picture is turned upside down and inside out.

During the last 30 years, it seems that children have been pulled away from their families for many reasons because of our changing culture. For example, in western cultures we have seen a rise in individualistic values and social norms about family structure and relationships have changed which leads to different expectations about parental roles and intergenerational relationships.[18]

---

18 Twenge, J.M., & Campbell, W.K. (2010) "The Narcissism epidemic: Living in the age of entitlement," Free Press.

Also due to economics, millennials are having delayed milestones in life which in cases can strain parental relationships.[19] Higher education has also caused a divide in generations with different worldwide views also creating a gap. Not to mention already strained family dynamics such as unhealed past hurts can create a lasting barrier to closeness.[20]

Some people have excellent relationships with their children and they may support you through the horrible battle that will be your divorce and then some will side with the other parent and join them in the smear campaign that will come.

I have heard all of the situations many times from others and it is heartbreaking, but you will survive if you begin to heal yourself and possibly for once put yourself first, be selfish, and care for yourself as your number one priority. Adult children, no matter what camp they fall into, can and should work through this life change on their own. Maintain your relationships as best you can, but please do not discuss the divorce at an intimate level you would with a friend or therapist (although your covert may). I believe as we heal and grow through this, we give others around us a map of how to handle and process hard times that will inevitably come for all of us.

I have learned a lot about my life by looking back and reflecting on the challenges I had during my marriage. In my experience, my daughter had medical challenges that I was left to deal with without her father and I only had family trying to assist me. At

---

19 Fry, R. (2017) "Millennials are the largest generation in the US labor force," PEW Research Center.

20 Segrin, C., Woszidlo, A., Givertz, M., Bauer, A., & Taylor Murphy, M. (2012). "The association between overparenting, parent-child communication, and entitlement and adaptive traits in adult children," Family Relations.

four years old after her third eye surgery, my daughter had a horrible reaction to anesthesia, but we were sent home to wait it out. In a few months, she started to develop strange habits and I had no idea what was happening. Now, we refer to the disorder as OCD. I alone managed a recovering child and doctor appointments as well as the home, a part-time job, and eventually the mental health issues she developed from the last surgery. I tried my best, but I had no idea that growing up in an alcoholic household with narcissists and empaths along with early childhood trauma of my own had caused me to have issues that were not treated or known to me. I tried my best but children deserve better. My husband came with the same baggage and we used religion and counseling etc., but were still not healed adults. He was able to manage me in the covert dance that they do, gaslighting me and lying about everything. The world I thought that I was in did not exist.

As a stay-at-home mom who worked part-time, my life was committed to my daughter and husband and I wanted so much better than the latchkey life for my child. I played, taught, read, snuggled, planned experiences, went to church, taught children's bible study, and tried to provide the best experiences for my child. In the background, I had no idea that a covert narcissist was secretly undermining that relationship.

Trying to get doctors to help, child therapists etc., and desensitizing therapy was all a challenge, and add to that an upcoming relocation across the country away from all my support and family.

I homeschooled for part of 1st grade to make an easy transition to a new school but still had challenges with my marriage and my child being a child and normal parental struggles were undermined and used to manipulate and control her. For example, if we were in an argument and I disciplined her, her father would say, "When Mommy's mad, just hide in your room until I get home." Daddy would come home and sit us both at the table as two children and lecture us. I protested and argued that he was taking away my parental authority and demeaning me to our daughter but after a few of these times, my daughter and my relationship was so strained. I went to therapy, and she and I were in counseling but the covert plan was to ruin that relationship as a child hearing the message that your mom is unsafe, daddy is the hero, and that brainwashing cannot be undone. Our life was a miserable challenge, and I still had no idea that this was the plan. As a teenager, she was unbearable, and my therapist had me "retreat and protect myself" as I was constantly being pushed into confrontations in my home and car with the intent of reacting to be blamed for it. We were accused of abuse when she was 15 because she wanted to sleep over with a group of friends and I wanted to talk to the parents. Her goal was to live in a detention center and have her freedom and as a friend told her it was great and we would need to pay for her until she was 23. This led to being hospitalized in psych wards a few times and a recovery program. After returning home when she was 17, her father's rule was "just stop saying 'Fu*k you to her,'" and she could not handle him sticking up for me and left.

Only during the discard and divorce process was I able to see this and understand why years of trying to repair our relationship, amends, apologies, gifts, and visits were not going to work. After my part of our divorce trial, my husband traveled to see her and got her to be a witness for him in the divorce. The issue was a misunderstanding of the date that I last saw her but the message to me was loud and clear. He had control over her. She stated under oath that she wanted nothing to do with me.

I hope and pray that nothing ever happens to you to break your heart this bad as adult child estrangement as this causes such guilt and shame, but with the epidemic we have seen of children and parental broken relationships. I wonder if it has to do with covert narcissism. I know it seems like a buzz word but as we learn of our traumas as children and can label our survival functions to that trauma words and labels come up helping one to heal.

If you are experiencing this, first know that you are not alone, in a Psychology Today article we find this is as common as divorce.

"Because studies use differently-sized samples and participants are of different ages, there's no real consensus on how prevalent estrangement is; it's also worth saying that sociologists and psychologists approach the subject differently. Richard Conti, in a 2015 study of undergraduate and graduate students (who were mainly female), found a very high percentage of estrangement: 26.6 percent reported extended periods of no-contact while 43.5 percent reported being estranged at some point, which would make it as common as divorce"[21]

---

21 https://www.psychologytoday.com/
us/blog/tech-support/202305/
no-adult-childparent-estrangement-isnt-a-fad

RESOURCES

BOOKS:

- *Done With The Crying: Help and Healing for Mothers of Estranged Adult Children*, by Sheri McGregor, MA.

YOUTUBE VIDEOS:

- *Handling Disrespect and Abuse from your Adult Alienated Child*, by Dr. Joshua Coleman on Family Divided
- *When to Stop Trying to Reconnect*, Reconnection Club Channel Episode 147
- *Rebuilding: The Power of Self Crae for Parents of Adult Estranged Children*, by Marie Morin on Family Divided

Title: When the Silence Grows: A Parent's Reflection on Estrangement[22]

Dear Diary,

Today, I sit by the window, tracing the raindrops as they race down the glass. The room feels emptier than ever, and the silence echoes louder than any argument we ever had. My child—once my little one, now an adult—has chosen to walk away.

How did we get here? Was it my fault? Theirs? Or perhaps life's cruel twists that led us down this path?

---

22 A letter from an article "4 Things We've Learned About Adult Child-Parent Estrangement" By Peg Streep

1. The Weight of Memories:

Every photograph on the mantelpiece tells a story. The toothless grin, the scraped knees, the late-night study sessions—I was there for it all. But somewhere along the way, our roles shifted. They became the guide, and I, the one who needed guidance.

Did I hold on too tightly? Did my love smother their independence? I wonder if they remember the bedtime stories, the whispered dreams, and the scraped elbows I kissed. Those memories weigh heavy on my heart.

2. The Unanswered Calls:

The phone sits on the kitchen counter, its screen dark. I've dialed their number countless times, only to hang up before it rings. Fear grips me—fear of rejection, of hearing their voice laced with anger or indifference.

What do I say? How do I bridge the chasm that has grown between us? The silence stretches like an unending road, and I am lost.

3. Regret and Remorse:

Regret is a bitter companion. I replay moments—the missed birthdays, the forgotten promises, and the times I prioritized work over bedtime stories. I wish I could turn back time, hold them close, and whisper, "I love you."

But apologies alone cannot mend what's broken. Forgiveness is elusive, and I wonder if they'll ever understand the depth of my remorse.

4. The Empty Chair:

At family gatherings, there's an empty chair—their absence palpable. Relatives exchange knowing glances, and I force a smile. "They're busy," I say. "They'll come next time."

But the truth is, I ache for their presence. The laughter we shared; the secrets whispered—it's all locked away in that empty room.

5. Holding On:

Some days, I cling to hope. Maybe they'll call, maybe they'll knock on the door. Perhaps forgiveness will find its way into their heart, and we'll rebuild what's shattered.

And so, I light a candle, send silent prayers into the night, and wait.

Tomorrow, I'll write another entry. Perhaps the rain will stop, and the sun will peek through the clouds. Maybe, just maybe, our story will find a new chapter—one of healing, understanding, and love.

With love,

A Parent

CHAPTER 10

THE DREADFUL PATH
THROUGH DIVORCE

When I got that call on October 22, 2022 with my spouse telling me, "I love you but not in love with you anymore." I asked what are we going to do? His answer was "We will be separated for two years and then we will file for divorce."

I always did as he said, but I had just signed to sell my home in Montana the day before and now I had no home except our retirement home. I had no control or access to any accounts other than the joint account. I quickly knew something was wrong and tried to discuss it with him but was always shut down and controlled. I started calling lawyers at that time. Another problem I encountered in searching for a lawyer in a small town was my spouse's company created a conflict of interest with every lawyer I spoke to except one.

Actually, my spouse's lawyer would have been mine if no conflict of interest existed. At trial, it was used against me saying I tried to block him from finding counsel when I could not find it for myself. Shortly after the discard as the money became a contentious issue and I was finally told the plan, told to go get a job and after two years I would get nothing, he would not give me my half of the sale of our home or let us pay off the retirement home.

The abuse during the process began in the discovery stage when I was accused of everything one can be accused of, even asking if I was living with someone (three months separated, I was not, but he was). I later could see how I was in a fight that I was not prepared for and had I known a few more things ahead of time, I could have made different decisions throughout my divorce. Would they change my outcome? I don't know yet because at 1.5 years in divorce process and six months after the final trial, we are going back to trial in a few months. So, we will see.

Our judicial system is archaic and is based on the old saying fight to the death. In the Book, How to Make Any Divorce Better, the author explains that it is ancient and outdated and caused bad behavior and bad actors in the divorce process.

My judge assigned mediation, but my spouse had no intention of settling. Still, I went in with a hopeful heart and a good head for numbers. My spouse only used it to find out what I wanted and when we proceeded to trial, everything I asked for was used against me and defended from their perspective. Each of us were on trial for six hours on two separate days as if we were murderers. I kept a clean and factual response while my spouse chose to use mediation information to bash my character in every aspect of my life and to counter my request for an estate split and support after 32 years of marriage.

It is horrendous, and I want to prepare you for this. All states in America have their pathways to divorce and you will find that the family court system is not set up to handle gray divorce. Particularly divorces with no children, high funds, and property to divide are a challenge in most states.

All states have a no-fault choice, but please do not be fooled into thinking that your spouse will not try to attribute fault and destroy your character in court. The following is the main process of a divorce:

SEPARATION

Some states require separation before filing for divorce. Please seek advice if you need financial support. I was living in Florida and he was in New Jersey, but I filed in Montana because that was where my residency was and I had an immediate need to preserve our marital estate. During the short separation, he stayed in an Airbnb and I was in the home we had planned to live in when retired. Our bills were paid as normal, but I was told I was on a two-year deadline and would receive no financial assistance from our marital estate. I filed for divorce 40 days after separation. I had been here before and did not want to be rolled over again. This was the second time he had said he wanted to leave me in this marriage and I wasn't going through this again. I was over it.

GROUNDS FOR DIVORCE

Each state has choices for why you are getting divorced and all offer no-fault. Please do not fool yourself into thinking no-fault will be a clean process with a covert narcissist or in a contentious divorce.

No-Fault reasons are:

- Irreconcilable differences
- Incompatibility
- Irretrievable breakdown

At Fault reasons are:

(The legal reasons for divorce can vary by state, but below are some of the most generally accepted for at fault divorce... check with your state)

- Adultery or cheating
- Bigamy
- Desertion
- Mental incapacity at the time of marriage
- Marriage between close relatives
- Impotence at the time of marriage
- Force or fraud in obtaining the marriage
- Criminal conviction and/or imprisonment
- Mental or physical abuse
- Drug or alcohol addiction
- Mental illness

No matter which way you file please be prepared to be gaslighted, smeared, and treated throughout by both your spouse and their lawyer. I am so sorry to say this, but the process is horrible in family court with a contentious partner.

FILING FOR DIVORCE

When you file depends on your circumstances. I felt all our funds would have been gone and I was right. At filing, my spouse showed we had three million in assets during discovery and three million more were found. If I had not filed so quickly, it would have all been gone. We never had money to help our only child buy a home or a car because all the money was being squirreled away for his retirement, without me! All the relocations and homes were bought well below our standard of living so he could hide money.

I don't know your situation, but if you have been discarded, I would talk to a lawyer who has experience with high-conflict divorce especially if you are divorcing a covert narcissist. In fact, talk to all of them, see who you like, ask friends for references. Do this for your research but do not do it to limit your spouse's chances of getting a lawyer.

SERVING PETITION FOR DIVORCE

There are choices here. You can have the local government deliver in person or deliver via email from your lawyer. My lawyer suggested email so as not to embarrass my spouse at his work.

I am sure each area has their way of handling it, but discuss it with your lawyer. My spouse did not know I was filing but because of the financial situation changing so fast, I felt it would protect the marital estate, and boy, was I right.

If you can let them know prior, that may soften the blow, but in my case it would still have been contentious. I received a threatening letter after filing where he stated he would reveal all about us and this was my last chance to deal with him. I chose my lawyer. Although I took precautions not to embarrass him, he still brought it up at trial that he got it in an email. The point is, if they can make you look bad, they will try, so be thorough with your plans and lawyer.

RESPONSE OR DEFAULT DIVORCE

This is where your spouse replies to the court that they know you have filed for divorce and they have received the paperwork.

After this, I received a letter with secretive (dog whistles) threatening me that if I went through with this, all my secrets would be revealed. Think about that for a moment... the person who knows everything about you threatens to expose all your weaknesses.

TEMPORARY HEARINGS

These are things that you need addressed immediately like housing, funds for living etc. Talk to your lawyer about any and all of your needs in your situation and they will file correctly for you.

DISCOVERY/ PREPARATION

Your discovery is a set of questions set by each state that will ask about your living situation, possessions, accounts, real estate, and any personal attack one can think of. One question on my discovery was, "Am I living with anyone?" Another was, "Did I commit fraud by tricking my husband to marry me?"

A woman in my support group's husband asked in their discovery if she "touched the kids inappropriately." This let her know he was going to claim she abused her children in the trial. Know your numbers inside and out... you will be talking in numbers until you receive your divorce papers. Do various budget worksheets, know your monthly bills, and know your real estate investments, business information, retirement plans, and investments. Please see free resources on www.graydivorcesupportgroup.com

Please know what financial support you need to maintain your lifestyle or what you will need to do to be able to live the lifestyle as a single person. Keep or sell the home? Maintain boats and cars? What is worth the fight?

Seek free financial advice and please do not fall prey to financial advisors who charge just to meet. I am out 3000 dollars just to meet a few times to get nowhere with a financial divorce "specialist." Your bank and other financial institutes will offer free advice.

I caution your answers as we are told, "Just tell the truth," but truth be told, everything you respond to is being used against you to build a case and is even asked to anger and upset you. It is a horrible game being played and with hindsight, I would have played differently. Make sure your answers are short, direct, and truthful. Your lawyer can object to certain types of questions under the law of being inappropriate or harassing statements.

MEDIATION/ SETTLEMENT

Before mediation, I took a course titled "Divorce Negotiation Academy." It was well worth the investment. I have resources on my page to assist with this and offer what was not available to me at the time of mediation—a peer partner support through mediation and trial. My spouse negotiates for a living and I have not had that much experience. I learned to know what I want and how to present it, why I need it, and why I am entitled to my portion. My mediator felt my side was very strong but let me know the other side was, "Cheap and mean and had no plans to settle."

Mediation seems to work really well for no-conflict marriages, but in a high-conflict marriage with a covert narcissist, they mainly spend the money to find out what you want (because you know your numbers and you know what you need) to use against you in court. It is a horrible game plan but sad to say this seems to be acceptable and most family courts require mediation. Maybe you will get a compromise, which would end the process and the motion goes to the judge to sign off and issue your divorce decree.

I have heard horror stories that at this point some coverts still will not work with an agreed upon settlement, which will take you back to court at a later date after you file a motion for court assistance.

PRE/TRIAL DISCOVERY

A pre-trial discovery is a verbal interview with the opposing lawyer asking you questions about your answers on the initial discovery paperwork and any other information they feel they want to ask. Again, your lawyer is present and can object to inappropriate questions.

There is not a lot of information preparing you for this and the trial other than "tell the truth and keep your answers short."

Helpful information I have gathered from various sources are on my web page:www.graydivorcesupportgroup.com

TRIAL

Motions used throughout to communicate to the court are used to present new information in your case to the judge. Please be prepared for how negative and rude this communication will be about you, and you may also be smeared by the lawyer and spouse in motion to the judge

Example:

My lawyer and I filed to have bonus money added to the marital estate. We showed paperwork during the trial that this was built during the 30-year marriage and would be coming and my spouse only said it was not guaranteed.

The response was that I was a money-hungry and money-grabbing selfish person, using the court system to abuse my husband and wanted to prolong trial because I regretted filing so soon for divorce. Our response was redirected back to the law as an example and the evidence presented at trial and a reminder to the judge that I am being accused and called names in the motions, and it was inappropriate.

I include this example to show you that this gets ugly and I am never prepared enough for the responses. It emotionally sets me back and I need to recover all over again.

Please know that there is a very long wait in between these stages which includes no communication because your lawyer has no new information. It will cost you to keep calling and emailing at certain times.

SETTLEMENT

Hopefully it is close to what you want and need.

Journal Entry

May 21st-ish received another motion for them to reopen our seven-month unsettled divorce case. The motion is that the money my husband said would not be coming actually came from a bonus and after his $1 million bonus, $635,000 was deposited in our account, which he feels that I have no entitlement to. The court is willing to open the case to see what my entitlement is… It brings up the hurt that I feel from the respondent's lawyer decimating my relationship with my daughter in the courtroom just acting like an idiot. It hurts me and I rehearse everything that I wish that I could say on the stand, and it makes me cry all over again. You just never get used to this type of reaction and these motions coming through. You just never get used to this in your life because for weeks or months you feel calm and you get back to healing and you're focusing on yourself and moving on and then, boom, a big stop sign smacks you in the face and you're thrown back into this stadium, fighting with your bare fists for your life. It's horrible. It's stressful. It's disgusting, but it's one more thing that you have to go through to get to the end to get to what is fair and equitable. All that you can do is pray that the judge sees this, but they're all part of this game, all of them. It's like a theatrical show. It's horrible.

CHAPTER 11

WHAT NOW

Journal Entry

Committing to myself. No love relationships early in this divorce process. I need to unravel how this happened, how I got here, and hold myself accountable for my part.

Need healthy coping skills:

Call someone and tell them my thoughts, watch TV, do muscle tension exercises and breathing techniques for anxiety, perform self-care, take a shower, or get nails done.

Align with where I am today and ask, "Who do I want to be on the other side of this divorce?" My marriage and the system failed me.

Release the outcome. I need to clear the bench of useless players and share my story with everyone. I need to realize that I stayed with someone that was not emotionally available.

Metamorphosis
By Lyn Sayre

Divorce for some is reaching your end
For others it's sad devastation

The love you thought you shared together
Now leads to isolation

The person you trusted with everything,
Has left you alone & scared

You're lost & don't know where to turn
It's more than you can bare

Divorce is like a death to some
but There isn't a closure to it

It leaves you shocked & sad & alone
Until you resolve yourself to it

Then when you see what you've been blind to
You start to plan your new life

You pick yourself, up off the floor
And do what you think is right

And once you begin your new way of life
You can see your full potential

You find the you that was never there
That was treated as nonessential

When you reach the other side of divorce
You'll find who you really are

And that realization will give you the strength
to finally reach the stars

What now... When it's all done, final and complete, what do you want your life to look like? You can remember the person that you were or the person that you were with, but you do not want to repeat that. Think big dreams and get into the teeny tiny details because we get to focus on our wants and needs and create the actual life that we want. We don't want to let ourselves wallow in our self-pity and lose what life we have left to live.

In the beginning, I wanted to get through this divorce with grace and dignity. That was my mantra. I needed a figure that represented that and I chose Princess Diana... she held herself high with grace and dignity especially through a public (can you only imagine) divorce.

When I am down, I do a hard thing, something that I don't want to do. I take a shower. I pick out a nice outfit... you can be you or whoever else you want to be because you need to fake it until you make it. I stopped drinking and got a 12-step program with a sponsor years before my divorce. I also, through my divorce, have a counselor, a therapist, a psychiatrist, and I have not stopped working toward healing. I found that I had unhealed trauma and that's where I was living out of and that is what I'm working hard to overcome and heal. I made other big choices like, not today, and to remain celibate until my divorce is final so that I can focus on only me.

I'm going from survivor to thriver. I used tools to get out from under a covert gray rock; no contact.

In the book, *Forgive Your Damn Self*, there's a chapter called *Dirty Trauma*... in which she mentions the heartbreak that we experienced as, "so intense it throws you on the ground and kicks you in the gut and it feels like it has no end."

But we do have choices. One, we can build a wall and go into denial and blame or two we can walk through it and learn from it. She goes on to say that undealt with pain that is not transformed will become transmitted, and I find that so powerful because you can continue another relationship and the same things will continue to happen. Then, you will just be putting this pain onto someone else who has nothing to do with this at all. The hardest part to hear is that, "pain can be a gift as an opportunity to experience growth."

The biggest battle is in our heads. You need to keep taking the forgiveness pill daily... I heard a quote, I wrote it down, and stuck it on my refrigerator because it is so powerful.

It says:

"My mind is a wonderful servant but a horrible master."

There are a few books that I have read that I have shared to help with some of this trauma. There are a few programs that I've taken that I've shared to help with this trauma. Another thing that I looked at was called a self-care wheel suggesting that there are six areas in our lives that we need to balance out to make sure that we are living a healthy balanced life. The areas are professional, personal, spiritual, emotional, psychological, and physical. We have 24 hours in a day, and if you're being productive, the suggestions are eight hours of sleep, eight hours of work, and eight hours of play. I doubt any of us are getting anywhere close to eight hours of play. That's why when you look at your care wheel you should really analyze how much time you're spending on personal, emotional, and psychological healing.

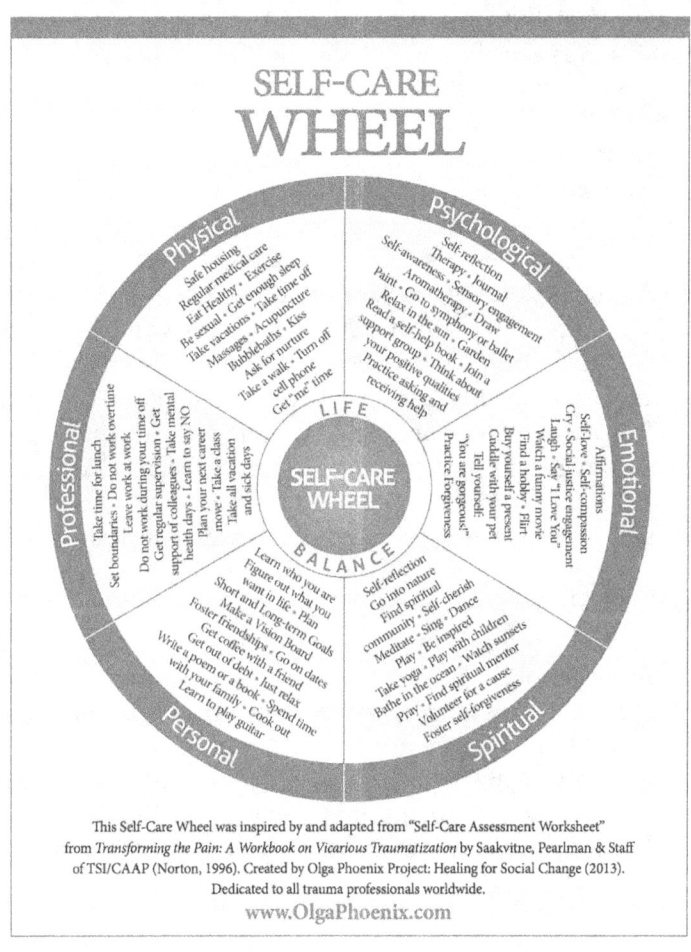

SELF-CARE
WHEEL

This Self-Care Wheel was inspired by and adapted from "Self-Care Assessment Worksheet"
from *Transforming the Pain: A Workbook on Vicarious Traumatization* by Saakvitne, Pearlman & Staff
of TSI/CAAP (Norton, 1996). Created by Olga Phoenix Project: Healing for Social Change (2013).
Dedicated to all trauma professionals worldwide.
www.OlgaPhoenix.com

We need to balance ourselves. It's not likely going to start with eight hours a day of play. You may add one hour of something like getting your nails done and add one hour of a walk with your dog or add one hour of going out to lunch with a friend. Add an hour of therapy to your week. Add an hour of reading a self-help book. Add an hour of gratitude, writing, and journaling. Add some time for and straightening up your personal space and making you feel good about your clothes and your closet etc. These are ways to balance out your care wheel.

Some people have given up their careers for their partners and it is so overwhelming to suddenly try to enter the workforce only to find out that you can make $15.00 an hour at 60 years old. Going in at entry level is very challenging. I have a suggestion and what helped me get back out into the world was to volunteer. I drive one day a week for *Meals on Wheels* and then I also volunteer with an animal rescue. Work on your physical self. Take some time to join a gym, get back into shape, take up pickleball lessons or take up Bocce Ball lessons. In the beginning, it's very hard to engage in these activities because you're depressed and you're feeling insecure, but it really does help to get out and volunteer and to be active and to start working on yourself.

I took a 12-week course with a church called "Reboot for Healing Your Trauma" and one of the biggest quotes they say there is, "You are not broken, you are wounded... and wounds heal with all the right steps, so think about when you get a cut versus when you break a bone. We are not broken from this experience that we're going through. We are wounded and we will heal if we do take the right steps. No matter if the divorce is your fault, your spouse's fault, both your faults or no one's fault. Whoever is at fault, all can be forgiven."

If you have a hard time looking at your part in the divorce that's something that you need to focus on and process. There were two people in this relationship and neither person is perfect. I used to say, "Even God forgives murderers." So, if God can forgive a murderer, God can forgive a housewife for the decisions that she's made.

One of the most important things that you can do at this point after reading this book and looking at some others, is to write out your story. You're reading mine right now. This is not the ending, this is just the beginning and your story will turn out beautiful, but it's good to tell the whole truth about everything. I have to tell you that in trauma therapy, to hear that I was abused changed my life because I always thought that everything was my fault, but to hear someone say what happened to me was not acceptable and that I was abused allowed me to start to process the hurt and the pain. Until then, I just looked at it as something that I did wrong or asked myself what I could have done better. I worried about this until I realized that this was a plan that was set in motion against me. I found out through the letter from my husband and that the way that I was treated within this marriage was abuse was a very helpful tool.

In the book, *Leave a Cheater, Gain a Life*, the Chump Lady (check out her website) is brutal and honest about understanding the truth about what we have gone through and will survive. What is healing? The answer to that is to make well again... not as we were before and not an old version of ourselves. This version of you needs to be made well. A deep look into old unhealed hearts that we carry with us daily and heal those, that is where your process begins. During my healing, prior to my discard, I worked on a broken relationship with my child. During counseling afterwards, the memories of being hurt as a child came up and I remembered being molested as a very young child. This was then the focus of being vulnerable and now healing that hurt and open to see how the experience of that molded who I grew up to become. This healing is hard but so necessary for us to continue. The healing has to come from you. Part of healing is the part of sharing with people that care and then also writing about it. We also need to learn to re-parent ourselves. It's very important for us even if we feel that our childhood was great. We need to be the love and guidance for the child that lives within us.

A book that was very helpful for me through this period of healing was called, *Healing Your Inner Child* by Caldwell Ramsey. Why are we talking about childhood when we are in our senior years and suddenly being divorced by a covert narcissist? Because we have undealt with trauma, which when not transformed becomes transmuted. You will carry this with you, and this will become a part of all of your relationships. Our childhood traumas, no matter the size, form us and if we want to freely heal, that child needs to be seen and re-parented. I can see that at times in myself during this healing period. My inner child acts up. If you take time and journal, it will come to you and you can say to your inner child, "You're Okay. I will not abandon you and I will stay with you." Whatever your child needs to hear to feel comfortable begins to help your healing. I've also used various modalities to heal therapy, CBT, psychiatric psychiatry, and online based programs. I have achieved some healing and a lot of information... as I've mentioned before, I follow a 12-step program. There are many to choose from based on your preference. The structure and the support and the built-in information has been invaluable to me in my healing as I think it will be for your healing.

I have developed a female-based coaching program after attending and getting certification in a female-based recovery program because of how powerful the outcome is. I have started a gray divorce support group because when my search was going on for a support group, I found no support groups for divorced people anymore. There are single divorce groups, but that's a different type of divorce group. I work with people through divorce as a peer partner. I am not your lawyer. I am not your therapist. I come and be a friend who has knowledge of what you're going through and walk beside you through your divorce.

EPILOGUE

In choosing the role of a traditional wife, I took on a set of expectations that were both limiting and exhausting. I found myself responsible for all the household chores—from the cooking, cleaning, and laundry to managing every detail that kept our home running smoothly. I became the secretary of our lives, the planner of holidays, and the personal assistant who managed appointments, schedules, and social commitments, all while my husband was the sole breadwinner. His role was to work and provide financially, with leisure time carved out for golfing and other pursuits, while I was left to shoulder the endless, invisible labor of maintaining our lives. I was expected to always prioritize his needs over my own, often sacrificing my aspirations, desires, and even basic self-care to ensure he had the freedom to focus on his career and personal interests.

In this arrangement, my identity became entangled with the roles I played for him, and I lost sight of my own *personal* goals and passions. Now, as I think about my future, I realize that having someone live with me may never happen again. After years of being a traditional wife, I genuinely don't know how I would manage chores and work in a partnership without falling back into those old patterns. More importantly, I have come to understand that I am not interested in sex with a man again. I want to build a life that is centered on my own fulfillment, where my value isn't measured by what I can provide to a partner but by what I create for myself.

Dating, too, has changed dramatically, and I find that many men and women in their 50s and 60s are navigating this new landscape in ways that seem strange and unfamiliar to me. People seem to be carrying more baggage, seeking validation in odd places, or clinging to outdated ideas of what relationships should be.

My next book will explore the end of my divorce journey, the process of healing, and how I am moving forward in a way that feels authentic and empowering. It will be about reclaiming my life, discovering who I am beyond the confines of being a traditional wife, and redefining what it means to be whole and fulfilled on my own terms in a world that has moved on.

ACKNOWLEDGMENTS

Your circle can get really small during divorce but if you look closely, you can see the blessing and angels that are in your life supporting you through this whole ordeal.

First, I would like to thank my mom for always being there for me and who loves me more that life itself, I love and adore you too. Also, Atlanta, Lynda M., my dear aunt. Love you.

Secondly, My sponsor Ellen S. She has taught me so much about the program and myself and I would not be where I am, here and now, without her commitment for the last three years. Serenity over Calamity.

Grateful to my publisher Lil Barcaski whose belief in my work and encouragement has been a constant source of inspiration.

Clare Williamson for creative design and support... such a powerful woman.

Thank you to my neighbor, friend and beta reader Barb and her husband Duff, for endless reading, valuable input and honest critiques, breakfast, and moral support. I am so grateful for your friendship and support through this chapter of my life.

Holly, I bought your house and gained a friend. Thank you for your support.

To my lifelong friends, Kathy and Angel, knowing I have your love and support throughout the years means the world to me and I am blessed with your friendship. No matter the length of time, it's like no time has passed.

To a great writer, Lynn, thank you for your friendship, support, and the beautiful poem you wrote for the book. I hope the world gets to read more of your beautiful writing.

Thank you to beautiful mother-daughter team Melinda Joy and Kim from the Shamanic Institute for opening up my creativity and adding love and light in my life through your friendship.

To my friend Diana, thank you for the soft touch and your listening heart. Your support keeps me going.

Caitlin and her beautiful family. Like a daughter and a friend I appreciate you!

Nikki, your counseling helped me to process one of the biggest heartaches in my life. Without your support and guidance, I could not have the skills to survive this heartbreak. Thank you for always being there with such a caring and pure heart.

Pam, my fellow Meals on Wheels volunteer and friend. You invited me in and took me under your wing. I appreciate your wisdom and Jersey spirit.

Juan Lopez, my sounding board and strong guide through these two years of trying times. Thank you for your heart, for what you do, and how you help others.

Maryanna Ostapenko, such a sweet soul with compassion to help others with their struggles.

Roberta, to the best damn realtor in the Venice Beach area. Thanks for all your knowledge, friendship and help.

Joanna Dahlseid, *Money Before Men* and the *Divorce Negotiation Academy*, you are a dynamo and your information and programs have given me the power to stand up for myself through this divorce.

Vikki Stark, *Runaway Husbands*, I am so thankful that this was the first book I found after my discard. Vikki is helpful to so many women and her program gave me wings to move on.

Evan and Jenny Owens, *Reboot Trauma Workshop*, what a wonderful couple and their program that helped me process past trauma and work healthily through my current trauma.

Jessica McKnight Photography, thank you for the wonderful experience and the beautiful photos.

Daniel Ball, thank you for being professional and handling my case with integrity. Kayla, thank for all your help. You both make a great team.

WILL THE DEATH OF US BE THE DEATH OF ME?

ABOUT THE AUTHOR

Michelle Lorraine always believed that life is an adventure and her journey is a testament to that philosophy. Having lived in a dozen cities and worked various roles, ranging from 5th grade teacher to TSA agent, Michelle has gathered a wealth of experiences that have add ed to her compassion for others.

During her 32-year marriage, Michelle was a stay-at-home mom who transitioned to a corporate wife, relocating five times for her husband's career. Whether it's the beautiful vistas of Palos Verdes, California, the cobbled streets of New Orleans, Louisiana, the mountains of Montana or the beaches of the Jersey Shore, every place she called home left an indelible mark on Michelle's soul.

It took years to earn her BS in English Education only to never have the chance to enjoy a career herself. Still, the desire to write was always a part of Michelle's daily life though her journaling. The decision to write a book on such a private experience came from meeting so many other women who have experienced the same issues with the divorce discard and court system problems she has been through. All of these women have gone through this painful process with no guidance so Michelle knew she had to help them if she could.

Now, working with women as a peer partner, Michelle partners with other women going through contentious divorces and is starting a Gray Divorce Support Group in hopes to help every woman in these situations not only survive but thrive and be the best person they can be.

Michelle resides in Venice, Florida with her dog, Carly Jane, and she enjoys going to the dog beach, listening to powerful audiobooks, and taking road trips.

www.ingramcontent.com/pod-product-compliance
Lightning Source LLC
Chambersburg PA
CBHW071010120626
46546CB00003B/1019